Your Blueprint for
PURPOSE

BMD Publishing
A division of Market Domination LLC

www.MarketDominationLLC.com
BMDPublishing@MarketDominationLLC.com

Copyright © 2024 John Creekmur, CFP®
Your Blueprint for Purpose:
Build the Life You've Always Dreamed About

All rights reserved.

Sale of this book without a front cover may be unauthorized. If this book is coverless, it may have been reported to the publisher as "unsold or destroyed" and neither the author nor the publisher has received payment for it.

No part of this publication may be reproduced, stored in a retrieval system, or transmitted in any form or by any means, electronic, mechanical, photocopying, recording, or otherwise, without the prior written permission of the Publisher. Requests to the Publisher for permission should be sent to BMD Publishing, 5888 Main Street, Suite 200, Williamsville, NY 14221.

Investment advisory services offered only by duly registered individuals through Creekmur Asset Management, LLC (CAM LLC), a Registered Investment Adviser. None of this material constitutes financial, legal, tax or any other professional advice and should not be used as the basis of any individual's personal decisions.

Printed in the United States of America
ISBN # 9798343327434

BMD PUBLISHING CEO - SETH GREENE
EDITORIAL MANAGEMENT BY CORINA AMBROSE
BOOK DESIGN & LAYOUT BY KRISTIN WILLIAMS

Your Blueprint for PURPOSE

Build the Life You've Always Dreamed About

John Creekmur, CFP®

BMD PUBLISHING

Contents

Acknowledgments ix
Introduction 1
Meet John Creekmur 3

1   **Brian Gareau**   13
Align Core Values for Fulfilling Life

2   **Pam Bates**   29
From Grief to Growth: Empowering Widows to Thrive

3   **Jeff Badu**   43
Tax Saving Strategies for Building Wealth

4   **Jennifer Cain Birkmose**   55
Trusted Services for Seniors

5   **Julie Kolodziej, J.D.**   71
Proactive Estate Planning for Smooth Transitions

6   **Michelle Kooi, CPA, CPCC/ACC**   87
Comprehensive Planning for Retirement Bliss

7   **Natalie Perry, J.D., CPA**   99
Legacy Matters: Exploring Estate Planning

8   **Babs Plunkett**   115
How to Find Joy in Life as an Empty Nester

9   **Nancy Schwartz**   129
Transform Health into Retirement Wealth

10   **Terry Tucker**   143
Embracing Everyday: A Story of Hope

11 **Scott Witzig** 157
Gathering, Growing, & Granting for Community Impact

12 **Stephanie Zepeda, Ph.D, LMFT-S** 173
Building Trust & Financial Transparency

Next Steps **187**

Acknowledgments

"A man only learns in two ways, one by reading, and the other by association with smarter people."

—WILL ROGERS

THROUGHOUT ALL OF LIFE, we encounter many people. Their stories, their beliefs, their upbringing, and all the things in life that they have encountered, are what have shaped them into who they are, at the moment in which you encounter them.

My life is the sum composition of the people that I have encountered every day. These people have shaped my thoughts, my goals, and my dreams. Some of those people you will meet on the pages of this book, and others you have met by listening to all of the guests on Great Decisions, Incredible Lives.

However, some of those that have impacted this journey the most, you have never met. I have much appreciation and admiration for them. Maybe one day, you will have the pleasure of meeting them also. Some of them are mentioned below.

This journey of turning our podcast into the book that you have in your hands has been long, with many hours of thought, work, and hopefully not too many tears.

My wife Stacy, thank you for your never-ending encouragement to me to take these encounters and communicate them to as many people as possible to impact countless lives. Your dedication to our joint passion of helping people to live incredible lives inspires me.

Tracy Heine and Makenzie Pampinella, your dedication to our joint passions has been inspiring. By managing the messaging, consistency, and quality, you have created and driven a platform for change. Not just a channel for people to pass their time listening, but a catalyst for people to change their perspective, so that in their own way, with their unique views, passions, and personality, they can be people of impact.

The rest of the Creekmur Wealth Advisors Team, you are some of my greatest blessings. Your passion in your craft is so greatly surpassed by your drive to impact people, as they are building their own definition of True Wealth. The Blueprints that you have created for people are the foundational building blocks to execution.

Introduction

YOU MIGHT BE ASKING YOURSELF, "Why do I need to read a book about creating a blueprint for my future?" Maybe planning for the future and talking about money makes you feel uncomfortable. Maybe you're afraid of what a financial expert might tell you.

The fact of the matter is, everyone should have a blueprint to ensure that they can reach their goals and feel good about their financial future.

Even with everything I have learned about financial success and planning, I am constantly looking for new ways to help my clients build the future they have always dreamed about. That's why I interviewed different financial planning experts. Each chapter will provide you with expert information on ways to create your blueprint for your life.

Over the years, our approach has remained consistent: start with a plan. Just as we took the time to carefully plan and build our family home, we believe that financial planning should begin with a conversation about what's most important. True wealth, as we define it, encompasses more than just financial assets—it's about what gives you peace, joy, and fulfillment in life.

In writing this book, I wanted to share the wisdom gained from countless interviews and experiences, offering readers practical advice and inspiring stories. Each chapter reflects the insights of individuals who have navigated life's challenges and emerged with valuable lessons. How do you want to live your life from this point forward? This question is central to creating your own blueprint for the future.

By engaging with the stories and advice in this book, you'll be encouraged to define your next chapter. Whether it's structuring your investments, having important conversations, or finding new ways to connect with the world around you, this book aims to help you build a meaningful and fulfilling life.

Meet John Creekmur

EVERYTHING BEGINS WITH A STORY. How did we get here, why are we here, how to we move from here to accomplish what is most important in my life. Often times, I find the more that I understand about the journey of life that someone has walked, I can find more truth to help guide me on my way. Sometimes what not to do, and often times what to do.

I grew up in Central Illinois where my family was integrated into the community. My dad worked at Caterpillar Inc. as a data processor and ran their technology department for many years. He was also a pastor of a small church in the community and served in many areas, along with my mother. My grandparents on both sides were also very engaged and active in helping many people. I was raised in an environment where we always pursued excellence in what we did but were always mindful of other people, with a genuine desire to help them in whatever they did. I saw this modeled by my parents.

YOUR BLUEPRINT FOR PURPOSE

As I began high school, I became attracted to a wonderful young woman named Stacy. She was raised in a similar family setting, with parents in the educational field. Her family was known in the community for caring for others, as they had a history of taking in kids who were going through hard times. Stacy and I shared this common interest at heart, and we eventually got married. We recognized that everyone we met had incredible goals they wanted to accomplish, and we dedicated our lives to helping them however we could.

This philosophy led to our business, founded in January 1995, Creekmur Wealth Advisors, which was built on the same principles. We met people with huge goals and dreams—whether it was working on their marriage, raising their kids, planning for retirement, or giving money charitably—and decided to create a business that helped people accomplish their goals.

I started out with a large national firm and opened an office for them in the Chicago suburbs right after college. I completed my undergraduate degree in accounting and then started working for that firm. I stayed there for a little over a year. I recognized that I didn't like the big firm environment; it didn't sit well with me, which I think tied into my personal upbringing and philosophy. My core values started to shine through at a young age, and I recognized that things were different.

So, we moved back closer to home in Central Illinois, and I was recruited to help a small hometown community bank. I started an investment department there and stayed for about two years, building some wonderful relationships. After two years, we started our own firm in January of 1995.

MEET JOHN CREEKMUR

We're really blessed that Stacy and I work together and have been doing so since we started our business in '95. At the time, we homeschooled our three boys. Two of them now work in our business as well, making it truly a family affair. As the kids entered the school system and got closer to junior high, Stacy took a more active role in the business. She's extremely intelligent, highly accomplished, and possesses unbelievable skill sets. She could start her own business and do whatever she wanted, but she said I had the idea first.

We often get asked how we manage to work together and still stay married. Stacy's answer is that we each have our own lanes. When we're at work, we're focused on work and not on family matters. If we have a disagreement at home, she is excellent at segmenting her life and doesn't bring it to work. When we're home and enjoying our time away from work, we avoid talking about work-related issues. At work, we each have our own responsibilities, managing and looking after our areas well.

Within our organization, she recognizes my role as the CEO, where I cast the vision and give directions, and she plays a significant role in that process. Even though we're 50/50 owners, she acknowledges that at some point, the CEO must make a final decision. Her job is to execute on that decision, even if she doesn't entirely agree with it. She understands that you can't have two decision-makers. By staying in our own lanes and executing our roles well, we work together effectively.

True wealth, as we define it, encompasses all the things in life that money cannot buy, and that death cannot take away. This is a broad-based definition, and at the end of the day, it's different for everyone.

YOUR BLUEPRINT FOR PURPOSE

It really comes down to what drives you, what gives you peace, joy, and contentment. What lights a fire in your heart and makes your eyes glisten?

When we start to look at money, I recognized early on that many people would talk to us about wealth, which often meant money and possessions, such as land or financial assets. I noticed, however, a disconnect between people's stated values and their views on money. Those who executed their financial plans well and stayed the course without frequent adjustments had a better understanding of their core values and what was truly important to them.

We began creating plans that aligned financial decisions and actions with core values, ensuring that these values were the driving force behind their goals. This approach resonated with many people, as they realized they weren't just accumulating money in their 401(k) for the sole purpose of moving to Florida and playing golf. While part of their goal might include moving and playing golf, incorporating their core values made their plans more complete and meaningful.

We don't want to work with someone just to make money. We want to help people who have accumulated or are accumulating wealth and have various goals they need help planning for. We focus on four main areas: income planning, estate planning, tax planning, and investment planning. These are the foundational pillars we address with all our clients. Ideally, we are seeking individuals with a net worth of $1 million to $5 million and a household income of $250,000 or higher.

We like to work with people who have a realistic perspective on money.

MEET JOHN CREEKMUR

If someone is solely focused on achieving the highest rate of return or paying the least amount of taxes, they should look for a different advisor. Our ideal clients are those who understand the value of money as a tool to enable them to live an extraordinary life. They must appreciate that there are more important things in life than just money.

It is a mistake to have no financial plan at all, but we see it all too frequently. People go through life, raise families, work hard, engage in hobbies, and set money aside here and there in a haphazard fashion. Then, suddenly, they reach a point where they need to make important decisions, but there's no coordinated plan with everything fully integrated. According to the last AARP study, 83% of all pre-retirees have no income plan heading into retirement. Lack of financial planning is the number one mistake people make.

The second most common mistake is lacking an understanding of true risk in investment portfolios. When we sit down with people for the first time and start to analyze their investment portfolios, they are often shocked to see the true volatility in their accounts and what would happen in the next market downturn. Most people are unaware of how much they could lose. When we replay history and review recent market downturns, it confirms the potential dollar amount they could lose. They have no understanding of risk and often have more risk in their accounts than they are comfortable with. People like risk when the market is moving up, but they don't like it when the market is moving down. Typically, during a market upswing, they believe they understand risk, but that's not usually the case.

The third mistake is the lack of a tax plan to legally decrease the amount of taxes paid. Most people only engage in tax preparation, getting their taxes done each year, sending them in, and either paying what they owe or receiving a refund. They don't go through tax planning to legally decrease their total tax liability, however.

Many people lack clarity on what they truly want to achieve. The biggest challenge we help them with is defining their goals and objectives and gaining transparency on their desired direction. Once this is established, the next challenge is figuring out how to get there. Many people lack a blueprint or a map to guide them from their current situation to their desired destination. We help them create that roadmap or blueprint to build what they want or reach their goals.

People often don't know what their goals are or where they want to go, nor do they know how to get there. This lack of direction often stems from poor communication. When talking with a married couple or partners in a significant relationship, we find that there is often little in-depth communication about what is truly important to them. Overcoming these communication hurdles is crucial because without clear goals, it is challenging to make informed financial decisions, such as whether to buy or sell an investment or determine the appropriate tax strategy. If we don't address these initial hurdles, it becomes difficult for individuals to make wise financial decisions.

The way we like to view it is to have a conversation with people as if they're building a house. Stacy and I built our house in 2012, and we moved in that same year. We saved our pennies and bought a beautiful piece of farmland surrounded by woods. When we first sat down with

MEET JOHN CREEKMUR

the builder, his questions were not about the number of bedrooms or the square footage. Instead, he asked, "How do you envision living in this house? What do you want to do with this house?"

Over the course of a couple of hours, we communicated the things that were most important to us. We love family and our community, so we wanted a house that would allow us to live a life that included both. This influenced the open design of our kitchen, living room, and dining room, to accommodate large groups. Stacy and I also recognized that we might need to care for aging parents, so we designed the house with this in mind. We considered the number of bedrooms, the size of doorways, and the types of bathroom equipment to ensure the house could adapt to our needs. Additionally, we wanted our out-of-town family and friends to feel comfortable staying with us for extended periods.

I told the builder I wanted a fire pit outside where people could gather and a window in the kitchen to see what was happening around it. One of my fondest memories is of my dad, before he passed away, sitting around the fire pit with our teenage nieces and nephews having a conversation about character. That picture is ingrained in my mind.

During the construction, however, I noticed that the window we had discussed to look out over the fire pit wasn't in the plan. The carpenter confirmed that while we had talked about it, it wasn't on the blueprint. This was a stumbling block in realizing our vision. We went back and corrected it, which required reordering a special window and ended up costing a bit more. But making this adjustment allowed us to realize one of our dreams. Looking back over the last 12 years, we built a house where we hosted holidays, sometimes with 50 people, including community members and family. Our home has created countless memories.

Creating financial plans is like building a house. It's not just about laying the foundation, framing the walls, or doing the finishing touches. It all begins with a conversation about what's most important. Most people never have that conversation, but it is the key to identifying true wealth and building a financial plan that works for them. The best time to start having conversations about financial planning and wealth management is today. Often, people delay these conversations.

Everything—from running a business, building your organization, crafting a financial plan, to accomplishing goals—begins and ends with a plan. Without a plan, you won't achieve what you ultimately envision. The plan is essential. People often make investment decisions without a plan. They look at their 401(k) and might pick a fund, a strategy, or a target date, set it, and forget it. There is no plan driving those decisions.

At Creekmur Wealth Advisors, every single conversation is built around a plan. We have four types of meetings, and each one begins and ends with a plan. We always evaluate where the client is in achieving their goals.

When writing this book, I wanted to provide people with a collection of incredible stories and advice. Over the past year, we've gathered so many rich insights on financial planning from interviewing different experts. My hope is that people can easily read and take away

MEET JOHN CREEKMUR

actionable ideas to help them make better decisions.

I learned so much from each interview and was truly blown away by the insights they shared from their life experiences. Each person is on a unique journey, and hearing firsthand how they navigated challenges and adjusted along the way was profound. From these conversations emerged actionable steps that I am actively working on today.

Each one of the interviews, we have turned into a chapter in this book. I trust that you will find that each chapter leans upon the rich background of each speaker. As you read each chapter, you will notice a common thread. A question…"How do you want to live your life from this point forward?" Each speaker has contributed to a guidepath discussion that will challenge you to ask big questions of yourself. Taken together, our goal is to challenge you to begin the journey of defining the next chapter in your life.

From that definition, you can begin to put together a "BLUEPRINT" that will help guide your decisions as you build the next chapter of your life. How do you structure your investments? What conversations do you need to have? How do you need to engage with the world around you in a more meaningful way?

Six months ago, I finished the book, and as a result, I began reflecting on what is truly important to me. I started identifying the conversations I need to have and the people I need to engage with. Additionally, I began outlining the major life goals I aim to achieve. As a result of this process, I put together my own blueprint. I now find myself in a better place than I was before reading the book, because I have confidence in the next steps that I need to take to build the next stage of life.

My hope is that this book, and these interviews, will help readers gain a clear idea of how to begin financial planning and what kind of financial planning might be right for them.

Let's begin.

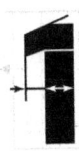

BRIAN GAREAU

Align Core Values for Fulfilling Life

YOUR BLUEPRINT FOR PURPOSE

LIVING AN INCREDIBLE LIFE sounds like an out of reach idealized fantasy. Yet, I have met thousands of people from all around the world that are truly living a life of joy, fulfillment, and impact. For each, it looks a bit different, but it is their journey, it is their definition of an incredible life. Even though each individual had different backgrounds, up-bringing's, financial status, and family status, they all had one thing in common.

Each one of them understand their true core values. They were able to identify what is truly important to them. They can describe what their life is centered on. Over the last 25 years, I have been able to get to know Brian Gareau. Brian is an accomplished corporate expert in organizational structure and performance. He has spent his life studying what causes a business, a not-for-profit, a church, a family, and a person to increase impact and bring about significant outcomes.

By following this chapter and answering some questions on your own, you will begin to develop a greater understanding of what your core values are and how you live them out. Brian shares from his life, examples of how he came to identify what is truly important to him, and how he is intentionally growing those values in the generations to come.

🎙 SCAN ME TO LISTEN TO BRIAN'S FULL INTERVIEW

John Creekmur: Brian, how long have we known each other? I was trying to think back the other day.

Brian Gareau: I think 20-plus years, easily. We met in a very nice office in the top of a barn. We've followed you all around since then.

John Creekmur: For those that weren't aware, 20-some years ago, we built a barn on our family farm and had our office there. That's when I first met Brian and Pat, and I've been with the Gareaus, goodness for now over 20 years. It's been a fun journey developing such great friends of ours. Brian and I get together every month for lunch now. Those are great conversations and I learn a lot. It's been a tremendous impact on my life, and I wanted to be able to share a lot about his personal journey in work and business and how he has identified his core values that have guided his decisions.

One of the things we always talk about with everybody is that we are on this journey to live an incredible life. Sometimes, folks listen to that and say, "You know, I don't have an incredible life. I'm pretty basic. This is regular living." Incredible living really means that you know what your core values are, and then you set your goals in the short term and long term for your life based upon those core values. Then, you sit down and walk through that with wise counselors. They set your financial resources to realize the goals you have, all the while making sure there's balance in your life and that you're living that incredible life. Often, there are distractions along the way.

Brian, can you tell us a bit about your career, your working life and what you've been doing since you retired from full-time work?

YOUR BLUEPRINT FOR PURPOSE

Brian Gareau: Most importantly, I was blessed for almost 36 years and married to a wonderful lady who's now watching over me from heaven. We have three adult children, each has a great spouse and there are seven grandchildren, two girls and five boys. One of our values that we talk about all the time is family. We are somewhat unique in that we all live within five minutes of each other, and we have a weekly family dinner together.

Family dinners are very flexible, given six working parents and seven very busy grandkids. For example, tomorrow night's family dinner needs to be super easy such as pizza or tacos because one grandson has his first flag football game. There will be 14 of us there rooting for one 5-year-old from the sidelines.

I grew up a thousand miles from here in the Adirondack Mountains of upstate New York. Actually, we were only seven miles from the Canadian border. My grandparents lived in the original homestead, which was built in the early 1900's. Then, after the Korean War, my parents built another house on the same property that was connected to the original homestead. So, a single door separated my maternal grandparents and my mom, dad, younger sister and me.

I had a great childhood and great family. I was very privileged to be the first to go to college in my family. I went to school five hours away instead of one hour away at a local university. From there, I moved to the Midwest and had a great 30-plus-year career at Caterpillar. I experienced things I never thought were possible for a small-town kid like me. Then, John, you helped us work out a plan, and I was fortunate enough to retire before age 55. But I couldn't turn my brain off, so I started a small consulting company. I also spent more time in a hobby – writing. I won't say I'm a great writer, but I love to tell stories. I've co-authored and/or authored nine books, and I'm enjoying life.

John Creekmur: You've written books that are used organizationally with nonprofits and businesses. You've also written children's books, and I think you have a goal objective of having a children's book for each one of your grandchildren, right?

Brian Gareau: Yes, I made a foolish public utterance. We had one grandchild at the time, and I thought it would be great if I would write a children's books for each one we would be blessed to have. I didn't know there were going to be seven over an eight-and-a-half-year period. I was blessed to release two more children's books in 2023 - that's six out of seven grandkids covered. I have some great people help me with editing and illustrations. Most importantly, there are some solid principles that I think apply to any child. One hundred percent of the proceeds of each book go to one of our local nonprofits, which operates a crisis nursery.

John Creekmur: It's a phenomenal way to stay engaged and to build the next generation. The first book I read by you was *A Slice of Life*. Is that the first book you wrote?

Brian Gareau: Yes, I was asked by another experienced author to co-write one. We've been friends now for thirty-plus years. We wrote that first book together and facilitated some fun workshops. The book is an allegory that takes place in a small pizza shop, but really talks about all those fundamental principles that are so important in life, one of which is to be actively engaged with family, friends, community, work, causes, etc.

What does that mean? It's all about your head, heart, hands, and habits. If you have discretionary time, that's where you're going to spend it. You're not going to take any ifs, ands or buts if you're committed to it. It's a story of a whole bunch of people in that small community that are engaged. Many of the stories are true – with a few name changes of course.

I think one of the reasons you and I have talked about that is there are more and more choices in life every day. Technology is giving us more and more options to consider. There's lots of factors influencing those decisions. How do we make better decisions? That's one reason we got together 20-some years ago. John, you led off our very first session talking about investing with values, not how much money we were going to make, but how were we going to live out our values. I think that's really important because you can do a lot of transactional things that inadvertently take us off course of our values. Values are like a compass and should always point to true north. We sometimes just think we have a better way and detour off course.

John Creekmur: You've recently launched a podcast called Latitude and in the first number of episodes you talk about a concept called return on culture.

There is an interesting thing to me. We hear about return on investments and return on assets but return on culture is a whole different concept. Can you walk through what return on culture means for an organization and why is that important?

Brian Gareau: I think the best place to start is with culture. You have a culture in a family. You have a culture in an organization. You have a culture in a community. It's simply the accepted or perceived way we do things and why we do them. I think we don't spend enough time talking about the why. But having been involved in a number of start-ups during my career and supported lots and lots of facilities around the world, the bottom line is it's easy to replicate things—buildings, technology, physical layout—but the heart and soul of any organization is its' people. How do we get them motivated? How do they feel valued? How do we create strong commitment? It's not a bunch of warm and fuzzy things as some people would say. There are some very strategic things to do.

One of the things that's really important with culture is to define what accountability means. I think that word has multiple definitions today, but we were able to see in the corporate world the huge benefits when we spent time on culture creating norms instead of just compliance. We saw improvements in quality, performance, attendance, retention, safety, etc.

I was fortunate enough to get to work in a Fortune 50 company where living our values and creating a high-performance, engaging culture were high priorities. They were considered 'need to dos' not 'nice to dos.' We saw some phenomenal results and not just bigger numbers. For example, living through the great recession, our CEO described it this way, "People were rolling up their sleeves and thinking about how they could make the company better." We had spent time building relationships, treating people as valuable resources and helping them grow and develop. We were living our values.

John Creekmur: You've seen it work as in the corporate world. Do you think the concept of return on culture is universal? Is that concept something which can be applied to a not-for-profit, to a church or even to a family setting or an individual setting?

Brian Gareau: Absolutely, yes. I've seen it applied. I've worked with nonprofits. I've worked with churches. People are people. Think about two families you know. One family, you're invited for dinner and the kids help set the table. Mom's not the only person doing the work. Everybody is very polite and after dinner, everybody helps clean up and there's great conversation around the table. Then, you have another family you're invited to visit and things are totally different, because the culture they've created is different. We do that in churches. We do that in nonprofit organizations. We do it in for-profit organizations. We do it in China; we do it in South Africa; we do it in Canada and in Peoria, Illinois.

John Creekmur: Earlier, you gave a definition of culture. Can you think through and repeat what your definition of culture was?

Brian Gareau: It's the accepted or perceived way that we do things and why. The first time I took some of my younger staff overseas and we were driving a vehicle, their comment was, "Why is the steering wheel on this side, and why do they drive on that side of the road? It's wrong." "No, that's the accepted way they do things here. They're not wrong. It's just a different culture." A lot of it comes down to values. We've talked many analogies for values, but there are several that stick in my mind. Values are a compass. They provide direction. It doesn't mean that you follow it, but they're providing the direction you said you wanted to go.

They're also the glue. The real test of values is not in the good times. It's when the challenging decisions have to be made. Even if you have really solid values, it doesn't mean you don't go through tough times or have tough challenges. It just means that you go through them and execute those with different behaviors. Values are also an important measurement. If you never use them as a measurement tool on how you're doing, then you tend to let outside influences tell you what success looks like and what it doesn't look like. Values are also like a magnet as well. They will definitely attract some people, whether it's an organization or family, but in some cases, magnets also repel and some people just won't feel comfortable in that environment.

John Creekmur: Let's say someone comes to us for retirement planning. That's an end goal for a lot of people. We encourage folks to take the old concept of retirement out of their mind's eye, if you will, to view it as a new stage of life and that their core values should be driving what that next stage of life looks like for them. Have you found ways for people to document their core values? Is there a process they can walk through that you have found?

Brian Gareau: If you grab *Slice of Life* and look at the back page, there are 10 fill-in-the-blank questions. I feel very confident that if you answer those 10 questions honestly, you probably could figure out your values quickly. That's my simple answer. But, it's not intended to be an advertisement.

John Creekmur: I love getting people to realize their values and where they have the highest level of engagement, giving them meat for personal reflection. That motivates me in our business more than money. The main thing I appreciate about all of your books is that it's not just your thoughts. You add questions and action points to make them interactive.

Brian Gareau: I like to ask questions. It's part of who I am. I think it's important if you're blessed with a spouse or a partner to really talk about what those values mean. Many times, people use the same words, but they're using different dictionaries. The more specific you can be, the better. For example, I got my car serviced today, just standard maintenance. When I picked up the car, there was a sheet of paper on the front seat with a little note that said, "Hi, we looked at your car. Here's the value of it. Here's a new one that's available. You can get a brand-new car for $70 less per-month than what you were paying before."

I have no car payment. But that was their logic - $70 less per-month than what you use to pay. A lot depends on how you define values and how you define success. For our family, vehicles were very much an important piece of transportation. That's it. What did that do? It caused us to make some decisions, like not having lots of debt and having car payments forever. That's not how everybody thinks. Another simple example was a house. It's a huge expenditure, but for us, a fancy, big house wasn't the objective; it was creating a 'home' where everyone felt welcomed. Those are some of the clarifications I think are so important because we throw out words, but they don't necessarily mean the same thing to everybody. I think especially with your spouse or your partner, it's really important that you have the same definitions.

Never forget that wonderful question that, as kids grow up, you get tired of hearing: "Why?" Why are we going to make that decision, or why are we considering that decision? I think that's really important because, as you know, helping us be good stewards of our resources for 20-plus years, you have short-term goals, you have medium-term goals, and you have long-term goals. When you start out, there are a lot of fundamental things you're trying to accomplish. As time goes on, you find that some of those things are less important, but perhaps making the memories is the most important thing. For us, the high priority was making lifetime memories.

We're blessed in that every year we get to spend a family vacation together. Spending a week together has a few challenges with 14 people in the same space. But the memories we're making, that's what life is about. For us, it's living one of our core values.

John Creekmur: You mentioned earlier about how values help whenever life does not go in a straight line. Can you explain how having the values understood by all parties within the relationship sets the culture up for success in decision-making?

Brian Gareau: I really have seen few things that are a straight line. Probably the best example I can give you relates to my bride getting diagnosed with pancreatic cancer and the 15 months she battled that and what we tried to do. We said in the beginning, "What boundaries are we going to set on where and what we will do to fight this terrible disease?" These had to align with our values.

Pancreatic cancer does not have any early warning detection (like breast or prostate cancers). It's actually called the 'silent killer' and is the third largest killer of cancers today. There aren't a ton of options at Stage 3 and 4. One of the things we quickly decided was we did not want to travel long distances. We wanted family close to not only support us but for us to support them through this life-changing challenge. That decision and the choices that followed were aligned to our core values. It's important to reiterate the defining moment in living your values is when tough choices must be made.

After Pat went to heaven, we discovered an amazing organization called PanCAN - the Pancreatic Cancer Action Network. They are the first organization dedicated to fighting pancreatic cancer in a comprehensive way. Its' Patient Services provides free, in-depth and personalized resources and information on pancreatic cancer. During COVID, by God's grace, I wrote Pat's story – *Keeping a Firm Grip – Perspectives During Challenging Times*. PanCAN received 100% of the proceeds.

As you know, it's not about getting resources and then burying them in the backyard. It's how we use them to help bring about positive change. Trying to be helpful to other organizations that are making a difference is really important to our family. Even though I'm flying without my wing-person today (Pat), those values haven't changed. That's how we're living them out.

John Creekmur: Having those conversations with yourself and with your spouse or partner is imperative. Those conversations should be driving your decisions. Often, we get to decision points, and we've not had those discussions, and then we're making decisions based upon whatever the field was in the moment, that does not help us live that confident, content, joy-filled life. It's a matter of making sure there's proper alignment on those principles.

Brian Gareau: One last thing I would like to say before we close our discussion about values is that everybody says they have values, but others can point out where they have seen inconsistencies. Here's a simple exercise called SAY-DO-GET.

First, we say our value is X – fill in the blank. Next, what did we specifically DO (tangible actions and behaviors) to live out that value? And ultimately, we GOT a positive result or perception. Now how about the flip side where your actions were inconsistent with our values or sent a potential mixed message? The result or perception of walking the talk diminishes. It sounds very simple, but if you have quality conversations, you'll find that you have many things that align with your values, and you can get even better if you look at those things that are occasionally and inadvertently misaligned. You will have richer conversations about WHY you made that exception and what to do if it happens again.

Below you will find the "Slices of Your Life Assessment" that will help you to better understand what is not only important to you, but also realize what you have set as your priorities.

Slices of Your Life Assessment

Fill in the blanks. What specific individual, group, activity, special cause, and/or organization would you identify for each of the following 10 questions?

1. I can always find time for _____
   _____.

YOUR BLUEPRINT FOR PURPOSE

2. I make no excuses (ifs, ands, or buts) when it comes to _____ _____.

3. I'm willing to go the distance, regardless of work or efforts for _____.

4. _____ is so important to me, that it doesn't matter who gets the credit for success.

5. My enthusiasm for _____ ___ gets others excited and/or interested.

6. When it comes to _____ _____, I can make the tough choices on my use of time, abilities, and resources.

7. I reprioritize what is important when _____ _____ has a need.

8. I am very willing to help _____ _____ with no strings attached.

9. Even if no one says anything, I'll do _____ because it means a lot to them.

10. There are no limitations on what I would do to help _____ _____.

Do you see a pattern in your answers?
Is it the engagement you ultimately want?

Brian Gareau is an Executive Partner at Magellan Executive Partners and the president/owner of Brian Gareau, Inc. After leaving his foreman job in manufacturing, he spent time in corporate headquarters and became a key spokesperson for all news media. Next, he moved to Dealer Services and serviced their North American independent dealer network with his team of more than 20 analysts. Brian and his coaching staff experimented with differentiating the workplace while maintaining local competitive wages.

Brian co-invented a patent-pending cultural assessment process (CAP). After leaving his corporate job, Brian became a Senior Fellow in Human Capital at The Conference Board.

Brian started a small, independent consulting business and has been a featured speaker at many trade association events, including ConExpo, NSSGA, AEM, and SIMA.

web | BrianGareauInc.com
email | Brian@BriangareauInc.com
phone | (309) 634 - 9137

PAM BATES

From Grief to Growth: Empowering Widows to Thrive

YOUR BLUEPRINT FOR PURPOSE

CORE VALUES CAN BE CENTERED AND TRUE, often living and impacting lives in a way that is common to all of us. We go through each day with no certainty of what the next will bring. Often times, we do not understand that we are already living an incredible life, and yet we are.

As we are all aware, life does not always move in a straight line. It zigs and zags. Often times taking us on a path that we never would have imagined. It is in those times, that we begin to realize that our core values are what is driving out decisions. We may sometimes have trouble seeing the next moment, the next day, or the next week, but we can know what is truly important to us.

Pam was living an incredible life with her husband, family, and grandchildren, in the small town that she had grown up in, then one day her life changed in a gut-wrenching way. In the midst of her desperation, her fears, and her pain, she decided… To Be Brave.

That decision to be brave has led to impact beyond measure.

Know your core values… Live your core values…

SCAN ME TO LISTEN TO PAM'S FULL INTERVIEW

PAM BATES

John Creekmur: Before we get into things, Pam, would you want to take a moment and introduce yourself to our readers? Then we'll start walking through your story.

Pam Bates: I'm Pam Bates. I lived in Galva for most of my life, and I just moved recently to be closer to my kids and grandkids. But I was in the dental field for my entire career and enjoyed that. About a year and a half ago, I decided I was ready to retire, so I talked to John and his team and said, "Is this possible?" They said it was, so that kind of made the decision, and I've gone from there.

I did become a widow in 2015. My husband of 34 years passed away. He was diagnosed and passed away three months later. We had a lot of hard conversations, but I feel good about the decisions I've made since he's passed. We'll go through that story as we go.

John Creekmur: How many children do you have?

Pam Bates: I have two, a daughter and a son.

John Creekmur: Great, and grandkids?

Pam Bates: My daughter has seven children.

John Creekmur: Whoa. Seven children?

Pam Bates: That's why I decided I needed to be closer: to be helpful. They go from 16 to 2.

John Creekmur: That's amazing. They're all close to you now that you've moved up, so that's incredible. You worked in the dental field for a long time, didn't you?

Pam Bates: I started in high school with a work-study job and then went away for a little bit for college and came back. I became the office manager and did that for quite a few years.

Then, we had a new dentist who came in and decided he wanted to expand, so he bought seven offices. When we got to about four offices, I said, "Okay, I need help." I was trying to coordinate them all, so we brought on someone to help me. I was a general manager for those seven offices for probably 10 years before I retired.

John Creekmur: That's a true commitment to one field, and I am sure you saw a lot of things working there. Was that all in Galva, Illinois?

Pam Bates: Yes. I worked in Galva the whole time. I was there for 43 years.

John Creekmur: For our readers, how would you describe Galva? Is it a huge, metropolitan area? Is it a rural community?

Pam Bates: It's a tiny little spot on the map, 2,300 people. There are a lot of farmers, and my husband was a farmer. That was the story. *The Most Amazing Harvest* kind of went viral when he was diagnosed and wasn't going to be able to harvest his crops.

All the farmers got together and did 450 acres in 10 hours. They had 12 combines lined up, and they had the trucks. Everybody was donating their time. The elevator, in fact, said it was Carl Bates Day and were only taking loads from our fields. It was just a big, beautiful picture of humanity, and that's what these small farming communities are like. Everybody just steps up and helps the next guy.

John Creekmur: I know that when the story came out, it gained a lot of traction. I remember seeing pictures of all the combines lined up going through the fields together. I know the ABC News did a section on it. When Carl was diagnosed, was it in the summertime?

Pam Bates: Yes, end of July.

John Creekmur: In Galva, Illinois, two or three months later, all the crops come down, and they work around the clock to do that. Pam, if we had one farmer working 450 acres, how long would it take for them to harvest that by themselves?

Pam Bates: I think that's probably a couple weeks to get it all done.

John Creekmur: Wow. A couple weeks of work, and he was diagnosed with a very aggressive form of cancer. There's no way he was going to be able to do that. How did the word get out about his diagnosis?

Pam Bates: It was actually his cousin, Dan Bates, with whom he did custom combining and that kind of thing. Dan coordinated the whole thing. It got to the point that they had to tell farmers, "Sorry, we already have too much help." People came forward with food and drinks for the farmers throughout the day.

Like I said, it was a beautiful picture of humanity, people coming through when they needed to.

John Creekmur: It's truly amazing testimony to the entire community of coming together to help out a family in a time of need. You wrote a book on that, didn't you?

Pam Bates: Yes. After Carl died, I felt it was God telling me to tell his story. I thought, "Well, you can't possibly mean me." I don't know the first thing about writing a book or telling a story like that.

Every time I would question, I would hear this song by Big Daddy Weave that said in the lyrics, "If you tell my story, they will hear hope." And I thought, "Okay, I think he really wants me to try this."

My twin sister had some writing experience, and so I called her and said, "Do you think we can do this?" On the first anniversary of his death, I thought I wanted to do something special, so that was when we started taking little book-writing trips.

It took us two and a half years to put it all together. But we wrote it, and initially we thought it'd be just a little spiral thing that we'd give our family. I told my daughter that, and she said, "Well, go big or go home." I thought, "Oh, for heaven's sakes, now we've got to try a little harder." We finished the project and thought we would self-publish it through Amazon. That was our plan.

A friend of mine had done that, so she gave me a company out of New York that helps you format it for Amazon. We made an appointment and had a call with him. He had seen the story when it was on the news.

He said, "Is there a reason you're going to self-publish?" We said, "Well, that's just what people have told us to do." And he said, "If you give me a couple of weeks, I want to find you a publisher." We said, "Okay."

He gave us a call back and said, "I have a publisher that wants to talk to you." We had an appointment with David Hancock, the founder of Morgan James Publishing. He and his wife had both seen the story as well. He said, "I want to say yes, but I have a team I have to run it by. We only take 140 nonfiction titles per year."

He went to his team, and they unanimously chose our book as one of the projects they wanted to take on. That was the journey of getting it all ready for publishing. It's a crazy story.

John Creekmur: Was writing the book a pretty big process?

Pam Bates: Yes, and there are all these things you don't even realize go into that, but they really broke it down. There's front matter and back matter and your testimonials. But they gave us a schedule, so it was a lot of learning new things, but it was broken down to the point that we got it done.

John Creekmur: If people want to buy a copy of the book, should they just go to your website, bravetwin.com?

Pam Bates: Yes, it's available there. There's a landing page called "Book."

John Creekmur: Nice. It seems like things have kind of grown from there. I also saw you have *The Most Amazing You*. Can you tell me about that?

Pam Bates: *The Most Amazing You* is kind of a book study for people in book clubs. It's on the website, and you can go back at your own pace to do each session.

Each session has a little bit about the book, and then we kind of talk about our stories and their stories. They can journal about their lives compared to the message for that particular week and then get back together and discuss what each person put on their little booklet.

John Creekmur: That's a phenomenal resource. So many people—me included—go to church and hear an incredible message and walk out and forget about it two days later. There's no accountability. There's no sharpening. There are no action steps to take. When I read books, I often walk away saying, "I wish I had a way of actually implementing this." This book study does just that.

Moving on, you mentioned earlier you have a twin sister. I also know the phrase "Brave Twin" means a lot to you. Where did that phrase come from?

Pam Bates: I don't know. The whole journey of becoming a widow makes you realize you have to be brave. There's a saying my sister and I heard one time in a crazy, silly movie: "Ten seconds of bravery can change your life or someone else's."

If you really think about that, you'll find it is true. It will change your life. You'll say or do the thing that could change somebody's life. That was the whole point behind the book and all the things we do. If we have made an impact on one person, we feel like we've succeeded.

John Creekmur: I love that. It's a huge challenge for all of us to recognize that in these short blips of time, we have decisions to be brave or not be brave, but those decisions can really have an impact not just on ourselves but on all the others around us.

I want to spend a bit of time talking about Braving Widowhood. It's a journey of life at this stage you're in, which is different than what I'm sure you had always thought about. Where did this idea of Braving Widowhood come from?

Pam Bates: The idea came from me being the only one I knew who was a widow. I felt alone. I felt like I didn't know who to talk to, so I searched for an organization of women who were also widows. I found one, but it was in Chicago, so I bravely made that trip to go to this meeting, and came home that night and thought, "This is crazy that I'm making this trip. Maybe I just need to do something back here."

With other widows, because you're on that shared journey, everybody gets it. You don't even have to talk about your journey. It's just being with them. It's like you connect because you know, and they know what this journey is like. That's how it started.

I went on a trip with these women from Chicago to Sheboygan, Wisconsin. I spent the weekend with them, and it was so much fun. Honestly, Braving Widowhood was meant to be for retreats. In a couple of weeks, we're going on our sixth retreat. We've been to Door County, Wisconsin. We've been to Saugatuck, Michigan. We've been to Galena, Illinois. We do some fun things. We usually have some meditations and faith-based things go on while we're there. The tagline of Braving Widowhood is, "Finding strength through faith and connection."

We're launching in November the BW Box, a subscription box members will get four times over the year. This stemmed from a lady whom I had just met when I became a widow. It was actually one of the hygienists in one of the offices we had. She asked for my address, and she sent me four grief booklets over the year that made you feel like you weren't crazy, because sometimes you feel like you're crazy in this journey. That was a really special thing for me. The boxes are based on that.

We have those booklets in each of the four boxes, and this is on our website too.

John Creekmur: Is loneliness common for women walking through this part of their journey?

Pam Bates: Yes. It's really sad. A lot of widows have had couple friends with their husbands, and they kind of fall away. They're not doing things with those friends anymore, and they eventually lose them. People don't realize those things happen.

John Creekmur: Is your group, Braving Widowhood, an open group for anyone to join?

Pam Bates: It's kind of an open group. We started out because we were going to do the retreats, and that was right about the time we had the pandemic, so we had Zoom calls. We don't do those as much anymore, but we try to plan something once a month. We've done movie nights. We have a newsletter that goes out to let people know what's happening and what we're doing, and everybody is welcome to join us.

John Creekmur: Excellent. I'm going to shift gears for a second. You and I met before this part of your story kind of began. We got to go do financial planning and to walk through retirement planning. Can you talk for a second about navigating finances after your husband passed away? Was that a challenge to do on your own?

Pam Bates: That's another part of that journey. You don't have your person to help you make decisions. Your kids are helpful, and that's good.

We had a farm, and we had an electric business, so what were we going to do with that? My son-in-law did Bates Electric for a little while, and then he got a job with the power company, so that went away.

Carl said to me before he passed, "If it doesn't make sense, don't keep farming thinking you have to do that for me." He helped me make that decision before he passed, which helped.

Like I said, I had you as a financial advisor before I really needed one. I can't even tell you how grateful I am for that, because every time one of those decisions came up, I would go to you and say, "Does this make sense? How should I do this?" and you were always very helpful in helping me get those things done.

John Creekmur: It's great to hear that. Let's say someone is walking through this life-stage change, becoming a widow or a widower. What are some important steps they should be thinking about right now?

Pam Bates: Have faith. God is with you. I can't stress that enough. Know that it's going to get better. Having relationships with other widows helps. Regardless of what the future looks like, you can connect with those ladies. Make sure you have people by your side, and everything will be alright.

PAM BATES

Pam Bates is the co-author of *The Most Amazing Harvest – The Man behind the Story*.

Pam lived in Galva her whole life until recently moving closer to her children and seven grandchildren. She was married to Carl for 34 years, and they farmed just outside of Galva. She worked at the dental office in Galva for 43 years, becoming general manager when they expanded to 7 office locations.

When Carl passed away in 2015, she and her twin sister were led by God to tell his story, leading to the publication of *The Most Amazing Harvest* in 2021. They then created Braving Widowhood, a nonprofit ministry to help widows find strength through faith and connection.

web | www.bravetwin.com
email | bravingwidowhood@gmail.com

JEFF BADU

Tax Saving Strategies for Building Wealth

YOUR BLUEPRINT FOR PURPOSE

AS YOU ARE WALKING AND EXECUTING the steps that are necessary to build your incredible life, there are hurdles along the way. When approaching a hurdle, you have 2 choices: either stand and allow the hurdle to block your path or find a way over or around the hurdles. One of those such hurdles is a threat to your financial security. It is an obstacle that many people simply say oh well, I cannot control it. That attitude and resignation has derailed countless numbers of people from realizing their incredible life. It has become an obstacle to heard, to move over or around.

Jeff Badu, a seasoned CPA, gives a passionate path forward. Not just to survive without strategy, but how to envision the next steps, how to logically educate and process actionable ways to legally navigate the nuances of the tax codes.

Often times, when I encounter people for the first time, and we begin discussing their ideal life, they focus on why they cannot get there. It may be a past experience, or a current situation with a job, or the money lost due to market movements, or the drain on taxes.

As you define and prioritize practical steps based upon your core values, all hurdles are simply an opportunity to move forward.

🎤 SCAN ME TO LISTEN TO JEFF'S FULL INTERVIEW

John Creekmur: Jeff Badu is a CPA with experience in business and real estate, both from the tax side and the consulting side. First, could you walk me through the differences between tax preparation, tax planning, and tax representation?

Jeff Badu: With tax preparation, you're filing your tax return so that you can be in compliance with the Internal Revenue code governed by the IRS. Tax preparation is a compliance-based service. Then, you have tax planning, which is a strategy-based service. That is coming up with different tax strategies. For example, you might change from a schedule C to an S corporation, something that's going to save you roughly 10% of your net profit on income taxes.

When we do the tax planning, we're going to use the plan that we create for the preparation so that we apply the strategies in order for you to avoid overpaying in income taxes. Then, we have the representation side. That's if you get in trouble with the IRS or if you owe back taxes. We can step in, represent you in front of the IRS, and settle the amount for a lower balance.

John Creekmur: So many people have that fear of getting an audit letter or of being in IRS jail, and so they don't really do much on the planning side. All they really do is get their taxes prepared every year. Have you seen people missing out on opportunities to save if all they're really focusing on is the preparation side?

Jeff Badu: We see opportunities all the time. If we have a client that has not utilized our services, there's a 99% chance there's something missing in terms of strategy. We see it time and time again. Examples include write-offs. We see a lot of write-offs not being claimed. For example, meals. As a business founder you can claim a pretty decent amount of your meals. We see a lot of that; that's one of the first line items we go to.

There's a rule known as the Augusta Rule, which basically allows you to rent your home from yourself to your business and write it off as a business expense. As the owner of the property, you don't have to claim the income. We see folks that come in with the schedule C's that have a net profit over $100,000. We could save you so much on the self-employment side, not just moving forward, but we can go back and amend the return from the past. We often see real estate investors not doing any cost segregation or accelerated depreciation.

John Creekmur: How far back can somebody amend a return?

Jeff Badu: It's typically three years from the date the return was originally due. For example, if your return was due April 15th, 2020, you have until April 15th, 2023 to amend it.

John Creekmur: You mentioned writing off meals. Stacy and I have a number of different businesses, and we host a lot of people for dinners and for parties. We have some land out in the country. We have a schedule C corporation. Are you saying we can actually rent the property from ourselves as individuals?

Jeff Badu: Basically, that is correct. The Augusta Rule allows you to have a meeting inside your home. It could be any type of meeting; it doesn't have to be a big retreat. It could be you having a meeting with a team member in your home or with your spouse who's your business partner. Maybe it's one of your monthly meetings to discuss business growth plans. Basically, the Augusta Rule allows you to rent your home to your business for up to 14 days a year, and the business gets to claim a tax deduction up to $1,000 per day. That's a $14,000 tax deduction the business is able to obtain. You, as the owner of the property, don't have to claim the $14,000 as income, because the Augusta Rule allows you to rent your home from yourself to your business, or anybody for that matter, for up to 14 days a year and not pay any income taxes.

John Creekmur: That is a huge tip, and that's probably only one countless things your team is able to bring to the table.

Jeff Badu: I would say it's one out of at least 100 things we can bring to the table.

John Creekmur: Incredible. Let's think this through now. You are in not just the preparation business, you also do planning. What can people expect if they walk through planning properly in terms of tax savings both short-term and long-term?

Jeff Badu: We structure our services in different ways that can get you short-term, immediate benefits. That's where we go back in and amend the return. For example, we had a client who had roughly $100,000 in self-employment net. Schedule C, that's the form we use for self-employed individuals. She does have an LLC, but she never was taught she could move to an S corporation. The first thing we did was an S-corp conversion, and it actually saved her about $14,000 in income taxes just from doing that conversion.

She came in thinking we could help her moving forward, but she didn't know we could go back and fix the stuff from the past. We also found out that she didn't have her business vehicle on the return. She had just bought a truck and drives two hours or so from business locations. That was missing on the return, so we found that for her. We used the Augusta Rule for her. Overall, we were able to give her back about $25,000 of what she paid in taxes. She's growing her business now.

That's a short-term benefit. But she can use those same strategies every year for the rest of her life, whether or not she utilizes our quarterly maintenance tax planning, because we've given her a strategy. In that way, short-term benefits can also be long-term benefits.

John Creekmur: What I hear you saying is that there's huge value in doing the one-time audit and saying, "Let's make sure things were done well in the past." But the real value comes with ongoing planning.

Jeff Badu: 1000%.

John Creekmur: We have a lot of readers who are W2 taxpayers. They might be saying, "Yeah, but what can a W2 taxpayer do? Are there some adjustments I can make on maybe some of my hobbies or some of the extra things that I do?" Maybe they're thinking about picking up a side job. Is there anything that might be beneficial for them currently as W2 taxpayers?

Jeff Badu: Nowadays, the world is so digital that almost everybody can be a consultant at something. You can become a life coach; you can become a business coach; you can drive for Uber; you can be an Amazon third-party retailer; you can do Amway. The beauty about this is it's so easy to start the list. If you're a W2 earner, you can start a side of business that can turn into a business, meaning you form an LLC or an INC corporation.

The moment you do that, you've just activated a whole new world of tax deductions. Now, you can deduct things you couldn't do as a W2 employee only. Now, you can write off your meals, your travel, your home office, your cell phone, and your internet. Use the Augusta Rule; have your 14 meetings in your house. All these different things now become deductible and help reduce your number one expense on the planet, which is income tax. We can start a side business and form it into an LLC and be able to use any losses to offset your income on your W2 side. An LLC stands for limited liability company, so it's a way to get you asset-protected, but mainly we're using it as a tax shelter to help you reduce your overall income tax liability.

John Creekmur: We have a friend whose company is called Under the Median because her husband had a job and she wanted to stay home while their kids were little, so they lived underneath the median standard of living. But then, she actually developed a consulting business for how to save money and find savings in your budget. Now, they have got over 250,000 subscribers on their YouTube channel.

They took something that was really just to give them supplemental income and turned into a big business, which has saved them on taxes.

Jeff, what have you seen with people once they walk through tax savings? You mentioned that your taxes are your largest expense. When people walk through savings, how much does that play into actual wealth creation?

Jeff Badu: At the end of the day, your budget is going to be very important. Your budget is composed of your income and expenses, which determines your disposable income. If you can reduce your expenses by reducing your taxes, that's going to give you more disposable income so you can fill up your asset bucket and start buying things like real estate. You can start investing in real estate so that you can build long-term, sustainable wealth and passive income. You can have more money to fund your IRA, your 401K, and your HSA, your college savings fund for your kids. This definitely translates into real dollars. We show our clients not just how much we can save them but what will happen if they take this money and invest it over time. Use the stock market as an example. What can $20,000 a year in savings actually turn into in about 30 years? A lot of money.

John Creekmur: It's a lot of money, without a doubt. Now, you had mentioned an acronym a little while ago, HSA. Personally, I've used an HSA for a long time. Can you walk through what you meant by the HSA? Why do you advocate for it?

Jeff Badu: HSA stands for Health Savings Account. It is an account that you can obtain either through your employer or on your own. Some people don't know this, but you can actually get one on your own. You just have to have a high-deductible medical plan, which is a plan that has a deductible of at least $1,500 or so, if you're single. This allows you to put up to $3,850 into your own Health Savings Account. Imagine you move money from pocket A to pocket B, and you get a tax deduction for that transaction. You put $3,850 into your own savings account for medical expenses, and you get a tax write off of $3,850. That's an instant return on investment. Let's say you're in a 30% tax bracket, but now that's a 30% return on your investment, a very high ROI in comparison to the stock market.

Speaking of the stock market, you can put that money into an investment account, whether it be stock, a mutual fund, or an exchange-rated fund, ETM, such as the S&P 500 index, for example. This money grows at the same rate as that index, and when it comes time for retirement, where you take out the money for medical expenses, you don't want to have to pay any income taxes on the money you put in or the money that accumulated over time. It's a triple tax benefit account, meaning you get a tax deduction for the money you put in, and when you take the money out, you take it out tax-free.

John Creekmur: Let's say you have a medical expense. Do you have to pull money out, or can you allow it to sit in there and compound? Is there an amount of time it has to sit there before you can pull it out?

Jeff Badu: Let's say you're 30 years old right now, you just got an HSA, and you want to retire at age 70. You don't want to touch any of the money in your HSA for that 40-year time period. Instead, you can tally up your receipts and medical expenses for that period in a spreadsheet. Then, send that report to the HSA, and they will send you a check or do ACH to reimburse you one time for all your medical expenses.

John Creekmur: That's a huge tip. To anyone reading, make sure you tell your advisor to walk through that, because that's huge savings. Can you walk us through the tax impact of real estate. Why is it significant for overall wealth creation?

Jeff Badu: With real estate, we can claim a tax deduction as depreciation, which is, in my opinion, the biggest tax deduction you'll ever get on your tax return. That can help offset other sources of income. Let me just walk you through a one-minute example. We have a client named Rihanna. Rihanna is 30 years old, she's a real estate agent, and she's a rising star. She makes $150,000 in her real estate business. She formed an LLC, did a great job there, and then she has tax write-offs of $50,000. That means her net income is $100,000. With no tax planning, she's going to pay self-employment tax. That's effectively 10%. It's really 15.3%, but we can knock off some points to break it down.

Then, we can also add a real estate to the mix to wipe out the entire bill of anything that's left over. Let's say she's in the 25% tax bracket. That's $25,000. Add the $10,000, that's $35,000. But she learned that she should be investing in the thing she sells the most: real estate. She converted to an S-corp, and she turned her balance down by $10,000. Then, she bought a piece of property using a Federal Housing Administration loan that allows you to buy up to a four-unit building with 3.5% down payment. She bought a four-unit building in Chicago for $400,000. She then could claim a tax deduction of up to 25% of the purchase price or $100,000.

Now, she gets a depreciation tax deduction. This is what we call accelerated depreciation of $100,000 that reduces her S-corp income by $100,000. Instead of writing a check of $35,000 to the government, she brings it all the way down to zero with one piece of property. She has a 3.5% down payment, and it's cash loaner $2,000 extra per month in that property that she can take to do other things with as well.

John Creekmur: That's an incredible strategy. I wonder, for those who aren't interested in managing rental properties, are there still benefits to passive real estate investing from a tax standpoint?

Jeff Badu: I would say you should try to be on the active side, where you're either a real estate agent or you own a lot of real estate. Maybe you do self-management, or you have a team of people you manage so that the properties are well-taken-care-of. That usually gives you the biggest tax deduction, because you can write off an unlimited amount. Whatever you get as expenses, you can write those off in full. However, if you want to maintain on the passive side, —maybe you dibble and dabble here and there and only own a few properties—you can claim up to $25,000 as a write-off.

Let's say you go through the accelerated appreciation like Rihanna, and you have a $100,000 available write-off. You can write off up to $25,000 each year. You can still get an up to $25,000 tax write-off each year by being a passive real estate investor

John Creekmur: Let me ask you a final question. If you could sit and have a 15-minute conversation with anybody living or dead, who would that convo be with, and why is that?

Jeff Badu: Warren Buffett would be the person I would want to meet. He's known as arguably the greatest investor of all time. I'd have a casual conversation and maybe ask him for some life lessons, like if he were to go back in time, what would he change? What would he do differently? I think the mistakes people make are sometimes the most important lessons they can give us.

Jeff Badu is a Licensed Certified Public Accountant (CPA) and the founder and CEO of Badu Enterprises, LLC, a multinational conglomerate that owns several key companies.

His marquee company is Badu Tax Services, LLC, a CPA firm specializing in tax preparation, tax planning and tax representation for individuals and businesses. Another key company is Badu Investments, LLC. This real estate investment company acquires residential and commercial rental properties in areas such as the South Side of Chicago to restore traditionally underserved areas.

Jeff aims to inspire and support the super-hungry to take hold of infinite resources to create an abundant lifestyle. He is extremely passionate about financial literacy and currently hosts various workshops nationwide. He is a public speaker, and his overall mission is straightforward: to make a lasting, positive impact in as many lives as possible, especially regarding their finances.

web | www.badutaxservices.com
email | jb@badutaxservices.com

JENNIFER CAIN BIRKMOSE

Trusted Services for Seniors

YOUR BLUEPRINT FOR PURPOSE

AS YOU STRIVE TO LIVE AN INCREDIBLE LIFE, you start thinking about the people who make your life an incredible one to live. In doing this, you start to think about the future and how, as you or your loved one's age, you start to require extra or more in-depth care. This can lead to re-evaluating or a change in your core values.

As you walk through this phase of life, it is crucial to start preparing for the future of not only yourself but our loved ones as well. Jennifer saw this need and decided to fulfill it. She is helping people every day to build a better tomorrow and a better future. Through technology and improvisation Jennifer and her team are transforming elder care and quality of life.

In this chapter you will explore how to prepare for the future with the use of technology and communication building all while making sure your core values are still intact, all thanks to Jennifer Cain Birkmose.

🎙 SCAN ME TO LISTEN TO JENNIFER'S FULL INTERVIEW

John Creekmur: Jennifer, you have an interesting background. Could you take a minute to share about that and let everyone know who you are?

Jennifer Cain Birkmose: I'm originally from Oregon. I'm a co-founder and CEO of a company here in West Chicagoland. It is a love letter to people who are older, who are looking to live at home longer. I actually don't live in the US; I live in Basel, Switzerland.

I, like so many people my age, have found myself in a situation where I'm raising children, and I have older adults in my life that I'm also caring for, even from a distance. This company is a love letter for all people like us who are wanting to care for our older adults from a distance. Why do I care? I have an 88-year-old father I want to care for, even from a distance. I've also had a long career as a healthcare executive, both as a diplomat in healthcare working for the World Health Organization and the World Bank abroad, but also as a longtime pharmaceutical executive where we developed drugs. I was a patient advocate driving patient access all over the world, and I'm still actually a board member on a company that develops all the malaria drugs we have in our global pipeline. It's a Bill Gates Foundation project.

All of those things bring me to this. The passion for healthcare, public health and making a difference has brought me here to open this company in Chicago.

John Creekmur: What an incredible story. You've got this background in diplomacy. You have a background with the World Health Organization and being an advocate there and in the pharmaceutical industry. But you've had some time at Second City as well.

Jennifer Cain Birkmose: Yes, that's right. I'm a Second City Improv and Conservatory graduate. That's probably the one thing your readers will remember: She's got some company in Chicago that takes care of old people, and she's a comedian.

John Creekmur: That's so great. My first introduction to Second City was in the 80s, and I absolutely love spending time there. They have a phenomenal impact with corporations in leadership development and leadership training. I know that had to have impacted you greatly over the years.

Jennifer Cain Birkmose: Definitely. For those of you who know improv or don't know improv, it's literally making something from nothing. You show up to a show, and you have your ensemble with you, and you get some words, and then you play it. It's alchemy. I think my great passion is actually what we call applied improv, where you take the lessons of improv and apply them to the lessons of corporate life or entrepreneurial life or, in our case, caregiver life. In our company, we've been teaching improv to elders themselves. I'm telling you, it is like watching Benjamin Button happen.

It's a gift really, to teach that and to watch what it does. Without exception, people become more present with each other, more creative, more open. We're shaking up that amygdala, and we're actually able to create some new wiring in our neurology and make new connections. You feel really connected to the people around you. You feel hyper-focused, and you have a good time. You laugh as a result. I really think it's a fundamental ingredient for all leadership as well, and very much so for caregiving. It's what we're seeing as we care for elders.

Our company provides a variety of different services in Chicago. We provide rides; we provide cleaning services and handymen and in-home tech and also food delivery. We teach our service providers improv techniques, and they use that with our customers. Our customers are raving fans. They're saying, "You always know who I am. You know my history. You always pick up the phone. I couldn't have done it without you. I couldn't have done it without VivaValet." It's so exciting. I love that we've brought these together, and I think we might see something in the future for us with Second City. Stay tuned.

John Creekmur: You kind mentioned incorporating some of the improv into the actual application of your guests and your hosts with your company. Have you seen some other examples of how your varied experiences have shaped your approach to creating and leading VivaValet?

Jennifer Cain Birkmose: One hundred percent. There's not a day when we're not using some of the techniques from the stage, even in our meetings. For example, using techniques to listen and to demonstrate that we're listening. If we're preparing for a pitch with an investor or a pitch with a future customer, we do character exercises to prepare, to make sure that we're comfortable, shaking it out. We use these tools to refine the storytelling, the physical presence and the biochemical presence.

The first rule of improv is, "Yes, and," so you agree with each other, and you keep building. In building a company, you've got to, "Yes and," your little heart out every single day. We have built entirely new business models for patient access in top-three global pharmaceutical companies that allowed us to launch products in emerging markets within 12 months of launching in the US using the tools of improv to get there.

We're using those same tools to create services, to create training for our service providers and to have outreach with our customers, because we have customer care calls just to make sure they're doing okay. A lot of adult children want to check in on our parents to ask, "Are you okay? How's it going?" We do that, and we use a lot of these techniques from improv while we're doing those calls as well. Again, the important thing is that it's fun, it's memorable, and people are having a good time.

John Creekmur: We've talked a little bit about philosophy, and we've talked about your background. Can you give us some clarity regarding your service offerings? What services does VivaValet provide, and in what locations do you work?

Jennifer Cain Birkmose: First of all, we're a tech company that delivers physical services. We are a digital concierge, so if you're like me, and you want to order this for your father or your mother or an elder in your life, you can sign up and use the digital concierge service. For example, when my dad was in the hospital, we knew we had to deliver services for him. Whom do you call? Whom do you trust to go into your parents' house? Whom do you trust to go and clean, if they need that during a specific time, or give them rides if they need to go to and from physical therapy? We're doing all this vetting with all our service providers to make sure these people are trustworthy.

We provide rides, assisted or normal. We do prepared food delivery, not like an Uber Eats, but food you would put in the refrigerator and have for a couple of days. We also cleaning services, and we have handyman and plumbing services. We also have in-home tech support. We've been doing cell phone workshops in Arlington Heights for the last seven months, and it's so popular. People love it so much, and they have a desire to learn. We've built this as something we can do inside the home as well. We are currently operating in Cook, DuPage, Kane and Lake Counties, all in Illinois.

John Creekmur: What are your thoughts for the future? Do you see yourself expanding outside of greater Chicagoland?

Jennifer Cain Birkmose: Definitely. We want this to be nationwide, because whenever we're talking to people like us, they're constantly saying, "Oh my gosh, when are you going to be in California?" "When are you going to be in Boston?" "When are you going to be in Kansas City?" "When are you going to be in Indiana? I need this for my parents." We know the demand is there. Our hope is to go as quickly as possible. We launched commercially in September in Arlington Heights and Palatine and Barrington, but now we've expanded to that entire population.

You could ask, "Why these communities?" We actually were digging into the census results looking for the highest concentrations of elders living alone without children living near them. This is a hot zone for that. A lot of people have grown up and moved away. That was the cut point for us. If you were living two hours away from your adult child, and you were living alone, very often widowed or separated or divorced, then you might need extra support. That's why we started here, and we're so pleased and so happy to be here.

John Creekmur: I can just think of maybe a hundred different families in the exact same situation you talked about in Chicagoland area, where the kids are living either out of state or in a different part of Illinois. With VivaValet, you are kind of revolutionizing the entire aging experience through the use of a technology platform and even bringing in some aids or assistance with technology into the home. Can you share the inspiration behind that platform and how you see it changing the way elders live their lives?

Jennifer Cain Birkmose: I love this question so much because it is like the beating heart of what we're doing. Why a digital platform? If you're going on a holiday, you would use Expedia or maybe Booking.com to have an easy experience. You wouldn't go to five different airlines or 20 different hotels. You'd go to this consolidation site, because that's where everything is. We wanted something that could give this suite of services that we knew elders would want. Before we designed any of the tech, we did actually two months of ethnography. That means we put cameras in people's homes. We did ethnographic research to understand your hopes, fears and dreams about how you want to live your life and how technology could make it easier for you.

We worked with these people to really identify if we were going to create an app or a website. What would that look like? They helped us design it. It's not just that we did it for them; we actually did it with them. We have user-experience testing all the time. They're actually in our team, so that means people from 70 to 92 are part of our testing and design teams. We make sure it's an easy-to-navigate interface. The silver economy is booming. We know that because of the research we did independently, but we also see that from the stats, from censuses, et cetera. It's the largest group of octogenarians we've ever seen in human history.

They have resources, they have time, they have their minds and they have their physical capability. They have purpose. We want to be able to continue to empower them with technology beyond our own sight. One of the things that has been a frustration is that so often people think elders and technology don't mix. I actually think that's a myth and a bias that we all need to start breaking actively on a daily basis.

John Creekmur: I totally agree.

Jennifer Cain Birkmose: Elders are curious. They're willing to learn all the time, especially around technology, and if we teach it in the way that they would like to learn, they're ready to go. I think there's a whole market for seniors that has not even been scratched.

Mariam Parineh and I were both on the UN Secretary General's Council on Aging. It's just kind of crazy. We were brought in to advise the Secretary General's office together with AARP to help come up with guidelines to develop tech for elders. How do you manage the digital space? How do you manage the broadband access? How do you design for elders? How do you make sure you have design inclusivity? We've actually been a part of writing those white papers. Those are on our website.

John Creekmur: We seem to be at this point of time when we see a lot of people leading longer and more vibrant lives. My mother-in-law, at 78 years old, is starting her own online sporting goods store and figuring out the tech for herself. We have all these initiatives. You mentioned the malaria venture. How do you see this intersection of global health initiatives and technology playing out and improving care for elders?

Jennifer Cain Birkmose: Global health, senior health and tech are all coming together. For the first time in history, we have these large populations who have a lot of reserves in terms of finance. They have the expectation to live longer. They have the will to live longer. They're feeling the sense of purpose, and the technology is finding ways to leapfrog a lot of the things we're trying to achieve. For example, in Africa, we have payment systems, remote monitoring and blood labs all able to be transmitted digitally. We can track weather patterns to more effectively forecast where we're going to have hot zones for malaria, where we have to have chemo prevention to protect the kids, the children under five, the children under 10 and also pregnant women.

In some cases, you don't have physical infrastructure to be able to actually even deliver the goods. Drone delivery is mitigating that. You've got new ways to do this and also new power sources in the form of solar as well as wind on the continent.

In terms of general tech, we have our step trackers. I have this beautiful Oura ring that I wear that measures my heartbeat right now and tells me how fast my heart is beating or my sleep quality. We are also bringing to market apps that will help you track your mood so you can have a more educated and prepared conversation with your doctor.

Obviously, digital medical records make it so much easier to be more transportable across the healthcare systems and across different care centers. But we see this all the time, and I think we're going to continue to see leaps and bounds in terms of digital biology and diagnostics, even augmented reality and virtual reality. Very likely in the future, why will people go to a place where a lot of sick people are if they have a well visit? You could stay home, put on your VR set and have your remote doctor consult you. That once sounded like a science fiction future, but it's now more and more of a reality that's coming to us, and it will benefit the elders so very much.

A huge concern we have in the US healthcare system is we're losing about a third of healthcare workers. That means doctors, nurses, all attendants, everyone who's actually in the system.

We're seeing a permanent exit between last year up to 2025 of about 30% because people are burned out after COVID. We need to have these new solutions that will actually leapfrog. We have these little robots that could actually be attendant robots, assisting us and our elders to get around and navigate safely in a home. It's also why we're positioned in this space, because we know that it's not only robots that will be providing these services; we need to find a way to mobilize our community.

One thing we're particularly proud of in our technology platform is that we're able to call up trustworthy, trusted, reliable services that can deliver for your elders. We're contracting people who know the community already, and we give them training. They have to go through training to care for elders, they have to pass exams, and they have to do test exams. We have all these background checks, and we're constantly checking to make sure they're safe. That's how we're using technology also to monitor our own people, our own services. Then, we give feedback. At the end of the visit, our service providers can say, "Hey, Mom's doing great today," or, "Actually, something was strange in Mom's house. There was a window that was broken. We're concerned. We need to let your kids know." We can give that information and feedback to the adult children to take action.

John Creekmur: I love that. I'm thinking about societal growth and generational trends. We know from 1946 to 1964, we had this baby boom population that was born. The front edge of that generation is pushing 78 years of age this year. Those born in 1964 are turning 60 this year. That age segment has influenced society every single step of the way. We know there are 10,000 people every day turning age 65 right now, and so that generation is going to be impactful.

Entrepreneurs like you have the opportunity to have an impact on one of the largest population segments ever born. I know we have a number of different CEOs of tech companies that listen to this show every week. What advice can you give them?

Jennifer Cain Birkmose: The advice I would give is, if you're going to be designing something with elders in mind, dream big. Pause for a moment with your idea in your head, go explore the problem that you're trying to solve and understand the reality of the customer you wish to serve. At VivaValet, instead of designing tech and writing code right away, we actually spent months working with elders at their eye level, watching them, observing them, talking to them and understanding their hopes, their dreams, their fears and how they want to interact with their communities and their families. We observed a lot of the "don't dos."

So often, people have said to me, "You're making tech for seniors. It means you just use a lot of big text." No, absolutely not. We're talking different neurological pathways. We're talking reducing choice, making clearer, cleaner interfaces. Also, if you're really in the tech space, and you want to start developing for seniors, please do go to our website, www.vivavalet.com and find the white papers we have from the UN where we've advised the UN Secretary General on how to design for elders. That's also part of the thought leadership we have. We've been doing the research, and we've been trying to get ahead of all of this.

John Creekmur: That's great advice for any entrepreneur, to really understand whom you're working with before you start. Is there anything else you want to leave with people?

Jennifer Cain Birkmose: Get involved in the elder space, and if you have an elder in your life, call them. We know the unhealthiest decision we can ever take in our life isn't smoking; it's actually retiring. When we retire, we often lose social connection, and we lose purpose. People are happy only when they have purpose, when they keep physically active, when they keep integrating in their communities.

If you can do one thing today, call your mom or your dad and say, "How are you doing?" Also, when you encounter an elder who maybe isn't your own relative, and that person's 78 years old, keep in mind they've also been 77 and 50 and 45 and 30 and 15, and a naughty 13-year-old walking around the backyard.

Very often, elders in our society become invisible. We look upon them with inconsequence. These people have won the genetic lottery to live this long, so we owe it to them to honor that and celebrate that. Enjoy them and celebrate the naughty teenager they were or the executive that they were at 40 or the person who was joyful at the age of 65 celebrating their first grandchild. All of those people live inside them. Honor that and see that in each elder. If we treat them better, we're going to be more integrated with them. We continue to learn more and also to treat them with more respect.

JENNIFER CAIN BIRKMOSE

Jennifer Cain Birkmose is co-founder of VivaValet, a service providing in-home services to help elders live at home longer.

Jennifer's experience of co-developing VivaValet's technology with elders through ethnography and a dual UI/UX experience landed Jennifer and her co-founder, Mariam Parineh, advisory spots on the United Nations + AARP commission on Age Tech. Always embracing the "Yes, and," mindset of her improv background, she has woven these concepts into her service model to incorporate service and understanding of elders with play and reverence.

Jennifer is the also the Director of Improv at Boutique Theatre in Basel, Switzerland, where she teaches and performs improv for actors and corporate training events. She holds a board position at the Medicines for Malaria Venture, a Gates-funded company that manages the global pipeline of Malaria drug development, solidifying her commitment to global health.

web | www.vivavalet.com
email | jcainbirkmose@gmail.com

5

JULIE KOLODZIEJ, J.D.

Proactive Estate Planning for Smooth Transitions

YOUR BLUEPRINT FOR PURPOSE

HAVE YOU EVER CONSIDERED WHAT HAPPENS as life changes? When the things that you have always centered on, the values that your daily decisions have been based upon, are no longer yours to make.

Many people do live an incredible life. They may not describe it as such, but they have been able to lay out core values and know them well, they have lived life as it zigs and zags- often times taking to places and in relationships that they never imagined, and yet I have spent time with them as they have lost mobility, or are entering the later stages of their lives. Often times what I see, is that the next generation of decision makers are not prepared to continue on making decisions of impact.

All of the life lived, impact delivered, and passion developed will end. It will end, without a strategic discussion, and direction. Julie has seen this play out in her own life and in the decades or working with people in helping not just create documents to deliver final wishes, but to create a strategic plan of lasting impact.

You to can have a strategic plan of lasting impact. Sounds daunting, it is really simple.

🎙 SCAN ME TO LISTEN TO JULIE'S FULL INTERVIEW

JULIE KOLODZIEJ, J.D.

John Creekmur: Julie Kolodziej is an estate planning attorney from the Chicagoland area. Julie, can you give us a bit about your background and the areas you focus on?

Julie Kolodziej: My practice has been focused on what happens when people become disabled and when they die, and how do you plan for those things from a legal perspective. If you were in that hospital bed, who might you want to make health decisions and financial decisions for you? Then, when you pass away, who's going to do all that wrapping up of the final affairs, and who gets what and on what basis?

I've been an attorney since 1996. I worked in a law firm setting for 20 of those years. In 2018, I decided I wanted to start a virtual law practice where I could use all the items of technology to make the process a little smoother for the clients. That was about a year before COVID. When COVID came around, I hit the ground running, and things have been getting better and better.

John Creekmur: You're a trendsetter. What's that experience like? Sometimes, people like to meet face-to-face, or that has been their only experience. How has the remote experience gone for clients?

Julie Kolodziej: We're from the Chicagoland area, so there's a lot of time spent in traffic. People are busy. It doesn't matter if you're 20, if you're 40 or if you're 80; things are busy. I think clients have appreciated having that efficiency. Personally, I'm willing to do meetings at seven o'clock in the morning or Saturday at 9 AM, because it's a little easier for me to do that too, so it's created a lot of flexibility where we can really accommodate the client's schedule.

I think they really appreciate the convenience. There's something about being in-person that a lot of people like, but for the most part, I think people are willing to give it a shot for an initial consultation, and then once they experience it, they really don't have any objection to the process.

John Creekmur: I think you're so right. There's just that convenience factor. It's so easy to sit down and have a quick Zoom call and walk through those questions and get the answers we need.

Julie Kolodziej: Also, I've been able to use the whiteboard to help clients visually. A lot of people are visual learners, and the whiteboard aids in clients' understanding of the estate planning process.

John Creekmur: A lot of people think they have an idea of what estate planning entails, and some people I've talked to say, "I'm not a Rockefeller, so do I really need to go through estate planning?" Can you walk through what estate planning is and why it might be important?

Julie Kolodziej: It starts when you're under age 18, in Illinois at least. Some other states have different exact ages. But before you turn that age of majority, you're presumed to be incompetent. There might be a lot of teenagers who object to that characterization, but from a legal perspective, the parent is the guardian of that young person. Now, when the person turns 18, or whatever the age is in your state, the light switch flips, and now they are presumed to be competent, and they have the right and the authority to make all their own decisions.

The first step in estate planning is dealing with health decisions and financial decisions in the event of disability. We've had situations where a college student might get hit by a car or have meningitis, or they're at the hospital, and their parents are 600 miles away and can't get any information. That's kind of the entry into estate planning. Everybody needs a healthcare power of attorney and a power of attorney for property and maybe even a medical authorization so the parents can find out what's going on when things are happening in that college context.

Moving forward, people start their lives, they get jobs, maybe they get married and have children. It is important for people who have young children to have guardianship nominations, and it's normally done in the context of the will. That's the next entry point. People might have somebody pass away or become disabled, and that event really triggers them to say, "I want to take care of all of this myself so I never put the people I love in a situation like this."

Then, we also do planning with trusts. There's a process called probate, which is the court process at the end of life where the family would have to go into the court, be in front of a judge and say, "Mom has passed away. We need to appoint an executor." There's expense and time and loopholes that are associated with that process which can be avoided. There are informal ways to avoid that process and more formal ways. Informal ways include joint tenancies and beneficiary designations. Trusts are a more formal way.

John Creekmur: A trust is a separate legal entity, right? I've talked to a number of clients over the years who've created trusts, but they've never done anything with the trusts. Is there a process they need to walk through to fund the trust?

Julie Kolodziej: A trust is a separate entity from the person who creates it, the grantor or the settlor of the trust. There are different roles in the trust. There's the trustee, who is the manager of the trust, and then there's the beneficiary of the trust, who is the person, people or entities that have the benefit of whatever is owned by the trust. There are different types of trust: irrevocable, revocable, special needs, descendants, etc.

The type of trust most people are talking about is called the revocable trust. The person who creates it is the grantor, the trustee, and the beneficiary, and they have right to revoke it at any time. It's really a pass-through entity. You sign it and now you have a trust. But there is a second step, as you mentioned, of funding the trust.

Funding the trust means we're either going to take assets and own them inside the trust as trustee, or we're going to name the trust as beneficiary on assets like life insurance, 401ks or even have bank accounts or stock accounts. It depends on which one you'd want to do, but there's still a benefit to creating the trust. You're going to have a will that pours over to it. Imagine the trust like a wine decanter and the will like a wine bottle. Whatever you have at your death that's not in your trust or payable to your trust pours into the top of that trust decanter.

Regardless of whether you fund your trust, there's still a benefit to doing it, because there are a lot of good provisions in the trust for your beneficiaries. There are things you can give them that you can't give to yourself, called creditor protected assets. They're protected from divorce, future ex daughters-in-law or sons-in-law. There are all sorts of contingency planning we can put in. That's a huge benefit of the trust, regardless of whether you fund it or not.

I advise my clients to fund it, and I give them specific instructions on how to do that, and I participate in that process with them as well, to help them get it done.

John Creekmur: You mentioned two different types of power of attorney: health and financial. Can you walk through the difference, and should the power of attorney be the same person for both those documents?

Julie Kolodziej: With the power of attorney, the person creating it is called the principal. Then there's the agent. The agent is chosen by the person creating it, nominated once that document is signed. With healthcare, the principal is deciding who to appoint as the agent to make health decisions for them. Most of the time, we're creating that as a durable power of attorney, which means that the agent will only begin to act if and when the person who creates becomes disabled. Hopefully, my clients go all the way through their lives and die peacefully in their beds many years in the future, and they never need to use that document, but it's a just-in-case document.

You're in the hospital bed. It could be a car accident; it could be many years in the future, and you're declining from old age incapacity. You can imagine who's in the room. Who might be doing well? Who communicates well? It's an emotional situation, and I help my clients think through the dynamics of that.

The second type of power of attorney is the power of attorney for property or finance, and in that document, again, the person creating it is called the principal, and they're naming an agent, maybe a successor agent, to act for them for financial reasons. If you can't make financial decisions for yourself, now somebody needs to go to your house, open your mail and pay your bills. That's what the power of attorney for property does.

John Creekmur: I find another big concern for people regarding estate planning is taxes. How does estate planning factor in the total taxes paid whenever a person passes away?

Julie Kolodziej: There are different types of taxes: income tax, gift tax and estate tax. For the most part, when we're dealing with trusts, we're dealing with either the gift or the estate tax. A trust itself is just a pass-through from an income tax perspective. You're going to get your 1099s and take them to your tax advisor the same way you do every year. For the person creating it, there's really no difference from an income tax perspective.

With gift and estate, that's really going to come into play when the person who creates it passes away. Whether they need to worry about that is dependent upon the state they're in. About half of the states have a state estate tax. Illinois does. Basically, we take a snapshot in time at the death of a person, and we say, "Do the assets this person has given away, during their lifetime or at their death exceed $4 million?" If the answer to that is yes, we're going to need to file an Illinois estate tax return. Estate tax will be paid on the amount over $4 million. If you're at $4,100,000, the $100,000 would be subject to estate tax, and it's a stepped tax, but, in Illinois, it ends up being around 16% of the amount over $4 million.

There are some states that have much lower exemptions. Some have million-dollar exemptions. Others have higher exemptions. People ask me, "What's the best way to avoid the Illinois estate tax?" The answer is, "Move to a state that does not have an estate tax." That is one good planning strategy.

Unfortunately, a lot of people have family in the State of Illinois, and while it would be nice to go visit someplace, they don't necessarily want to move and not be a part of those people's lives during that time. There is the federal estate tax. Right now, the exemption is north of $12 million per person. It's scheduled to sunset at the end of 2025, and we're not sure exactly what that's going to sunset to, or if they're just going to continue the current laws. We're kind of just playing a wait-and-see on that with a lot of clients.

John Creekmur: I had a client come in whose spouse had passed away. They were small business owners. I actually saw her get out of her car. It was a windy, rainy day, and she had everything in a paper bag and a shoebox, believe it or not. The wind blew, and all of her papers got blown around. She gathered it up and came in and said, "This is my estate planning." There was no trust work set up, no powers of attorney. In making final life decisions, it was a very challenging, emotional time with different opinions from the family. There were all of the business assets and business decisions, and none of that had played into it.

That was an extreme case where I saw a lot of the negative consequences you've mentioned hit one family all at the same time because of not walking through the estate planning. Now, they had a very complex situation because of the small businesses. But let's say an individual has a small business or a business of some kind, and it's treated differently. I'd like to hear your opinion from a personal standpoint. We have our businesses, the Creekmur companies, and we have two of our adult children that work for us. My wife, Stacy, and I run the organization together, and then we have one son who's not involved in the business. We're in multiple states, so it's a little more complex.

We're actually walking through our pre-estate-planning discussions right now. When you think about that situation, what is some counsel you can give to someone who is maybe a small business owner about what to be aware of when they're thinking about estate planning?

Julie Kolodziej: I deal with clients who have businesses, and sometimes entrepreneurs never think they're going to die. They're always worried about what's happening right now. But, as people get older and become less able to do these things, they do start thinking about business succession. There's estate planning and then there's business succession planning, and I really feel like you have to do both of those things at the same time. A lot of estate planning attorneys just do the estate plan and do not look at any of the business aspects.

Business succession planning can be challenging. Do you hire from within? Who's your successor? Is that somebody who works with you, a long-term employee? That might be a long-term employee who is a family member of yours. Maybe you're going to bring somebody from your family into the business. That would be a suitable thing for them, and they're going to grow up in the business. Determining whom that successor is can really complicate things, especially when it comes to family members.

You mentioned that in your business, there are family members who are involved and family members who aren't involved. Often, when we're doing planning, we're going to look at the business succession planning and the estate planning. How does this work? Who's getting what? Is it a gift? Are they buying it from the estate? Are we going to sell it to them now? Are we going to wait until we pass away to give it to them? There are a lot of different factors that go into that. For example, if you do have an estate tax situation for that business owner, where it's either a state estate tax or a federal estate tax that's going to be paid, now we get involved with estate tax. We have some capital gains issues. There are gifting issues.

There are a lot of different tax aspects, but in my practice at least, there are a lot of attorneys who just look at tax and that's all they do. They're going to try to force their clients into a certain path because of the tax aspect. With me, I like to listen to the clients, find out what's important to them and try to accommodate exactly what they want. I still plan for the taxes and advise them of those things, but sometimes other aspects of life are more important than the tax aspect.

For example, I'd sit down with you and your wife, and we'd talk about the family dynamics. I'd ask you to tell me all sorts of stuff about your children, how they get along. What was it like when they were 16, because it's not that much different when you're 50, or 60, or 70.

How does what we put in your estate plan affect their relationship after you're gone?

If you think fairness is important, what's your definition of fair? You have a child who's working in the business, and it wouldn't be what it is today except for that child, so do you give the business to that child? Or, if you don't have a lot of assets you're giving to the other children, might we buy life insurance? There are different ways to address that, but it's more about what the clients want to see happen. What's fair in their definition?

Is it an equal split? It's definitely important. Even if a business owner isn't ready to do business succession planning, I'd still go and do the estate planning. We can do it in layers. We do that base documents, and then we kind of build on it, get a little bit more complex. Now we bring in the business succession planning. We don't have to do it all right now. Sometimes, that complexity prevents people from even starting. Come in, get an appointment with an attorney, start the ball rolling, and you'll find out exactly what it is for you.

John Creekmur: I love how you phrase that. We're all individuals with individual needs. I outlined a situation with a client that came in for the first time, and things had not been planned well. Can you outline an ideal situation you might have experienced and what made it so successful?

Julie Kolodziej: I want to preface this by saying, no matter what, the dying process does have work associated with it. The estate planning process is about knowledge the client has within themselves that nobody else knows. Sometimes, that's not in such great order.

They have assets in a million different places. They have business complications, life insurance policies, stock certificates in the drawer whose worth you don't even know. The estate planning process is really about getting your house in order.

Getting your house in order might be consolidating assets, not having things all over the place. Once you create that trust, you do need to fund it. It's a good time to make a list of assets that you own, including life insurance. Get your important people around you—your accountant, your financial advisor, your attorney—all in one place. It's really an opportunity.

The trust funding process does allow us to do that. As attorneys, we work with financial advisors and accountants to make sure the clients do that. But with married couples, there's usually the financial person and the other who doesn't do any of that. There's the one who has all the passwords and knows where everything's at, and the other doesn't. That is actually a trigger as people get older. The one who's doing everything gets concerned, or the one who doesn't know everything gets concerned about what would happen if the other person dies. It sounds like that's what your client was experiencing. Estate planning is like a collecting of knowledge and also putting in place documents that will make it smooth for whoever is left behind. If that had happened, your client probably would've had a nice, neat binder rather than a lot of documents shoved in a shopping bag that blew across the parking lot.

John Creekmur: Thank you, Julie. Before we sign off, is there anything we've not covered so far that you would like to address?

Julie Kolodziej: The only thing I would say is that becoming disabled and dying is an emotional thing, and there's a lot going on. I can't tell you how many times I've had clients come in the month after their spouses passed away. It's a year later, and they don't even remember what we talked about. They didn't even know how emotional it was for them until they came out of it on the other side. The more you can do to make that as easy as possible through proper tax planning, financial planning and estate planning and maybe even business succession planning, the better. It's really a gift to your loved ones, creating organization from chaos.

JULIE KOLODZIEJ, J.D.

Julie Kolodziej, J.D., is a 1996 graduate of DePaul University College of Law with extensive expertise in estate planning, guardianship, probate, trust administration, and tax. She focuses on helping families create proactive plans to navigate life's challenges, ensuring that family relationships remain intact. Julie is driven by the experiences of families torn apart due to the lack of proper planning, motivating her to guide clients in preparing for potential disability and eventual death.

As the founder of the estate and trust administration and litigation practice at Matlin Law Group, P.C., Julie has been offering expert legal advice since 1998. Her early work at McDonald's Corporation taught her the importance of process and efficiency, skills she now applies to deliver consistent, high-quality legal solutions. Julie is passionate about educating clients, listening to their concerns, and crafting plans that reflect their true intentions with care and dedication.

web | www.jprlawgroup.com
email | julie@jprlawgroup.com
phone | (773) 245 - 5262

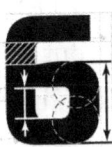

MICHELLE KOOI, CPA, CPCC/ACC

Comprehensive Planning For Retirement Bliss

YOUR BLUEPRINT FOR PURPOSE

OVERWHELMED, PROCRASTINATING, given to being an imposter. Have you ever felt that way? Often, there is the busyness of life, the demands of work, the drive of the world around us, and most importantly the unrealistic expectations of what we put on ourselves. All of this can take us off the path toward living an incredible life.

It doesn't have to be that way. You have the control and ability to change the dynamic. To focus your efforts on hitting the next stage of growth with confidence. Most times it takes change. Change of environment, change of location, change of relationships- But mostly it comes from a change of perspective.

Michelle is such a breath of fresh air as she has taken her personal life journey, her deep tax and accounting knowledge, her passion for impacting people, and her joyful perspective in life to change lives in a meaningful way, every day.

Aligning core values with practical steps might seem small, but they facilitate meaningful progress on your journey to living an incredible life.

🎙 SCAN ME TO LISTEN TO MICHELLE'S FULL INTERVIEW

MICHELLE KOOI, CPA, CPCC/ACC

John Creekmur: Michelle, you have a phenomenal background. Could you introduce yourself for us?

Michelle Kooi: I am the founder of Confluence Coaching and Consulting, which is a business that works with women overwhelmed in their businesses or work and helping them reconnect with themselves, reduce stress and get really clear on what's important so they can live life with more intention and joy and purpose.

I have spent the last 20 years as a CPA, working in public accounting, but I actually have a degree in journalism, which was my first degree. I worked for a number of years in sales, customer service, operations, environmental business, and a number of different things, but I wasn't really connected and enjoying what I was doing. I had always loved accounting, so I went back to school when my kids were young and got a degree in accounting. I've taught yoga. I have done a number of different things. But my favorite thing is connecting with my clients and understanding what is important to them and what makes them tick. Connecting them with themselves helps them manage their lives and their money better.

John Creekmur: When we first talked, I was blown away by how you have that technical background with the CPA work. It really allows you to understand how businesses and finances work together. It's that unusual melding of the technical aspects with the passionate heart of a coach or a teacher that fascinates me. It's not a perspective many people get to see.

Can you walk through how you see coaching and consulting services together and how that helps the individual navigate change?

The reason I want to talk about change is that oftentimes we go through life with expectations of how things will go, and then a wrench of change gets thrown our way. How can we walk through that coaching experience to help people navigate change?

Michelle Kooi: I love working with clients who are going through some sort of change or transition. Life is not static and it's not smooth. It's up and down. There is always going to be change. Change brings up the unknown; it brings up uncertainty, which can be scary. But it can also bring huge opportunity. We work with clients to dive into that, to trust themselves, to trust their higher power and to trust what they know and to also surround themselves with people who know things they don't. We help them become open to learning. We help them connect with themselves, as I said earlier, to be more authentic.

I work with people on a little bit of a somatic level. Being a CPA, I'm very left-brained. But I'm also very creative and right-brained. I bring those two together; I have the hard skills and the knowledge to walk them through budgeting or debt reduction or understanding their QuickBooks files, but on the other hand, I understand emotions, which is also important. So many people don't know what their values are. We'll work on that. We'll work on trust, trust with themselves, digging deep with themselves to connect to some past trauma or different experiences which have colored things so that they're reacting in a certain way that maybe doesn't make sense anymore. Maybe it did at one time, but it doesn't now.

We create a lot of awareness, which can really help with making those decisions but also helps them get out of their heads, because we can't always think through things. We need a different perspective, and that coaching aspect helps them see things from a different perspective and can help get them unstuck and moving forward.

John Creekmur: You mentioned that most people don't know what their core values are. Maybe they have an idea or a certain worldview that they operate on but they never phrase it that way. Are there some things you've learned in working with people to help them identify what those core values are?

Michelle Kooi: Yes. It could be anything from what they gravitate to, what they enjoy, what brings them joy, where they find themselves at their best. Getting feedback from other people can also help. I've had clients pull out bank statements and go through them to discover where they're spending their money. That can also show some values.

John Creekmur: That's a process I encourage everyone to walk through. Pick out your checking account statement or your debit card statement or credit card statement and write down what you spent money on. Often, that indicates where your heart is. We have this concept that everyone needs to know what their core values are and then properly align their goals with their core values.

Speaking of values, you said people should trust what they know. What did you mean by that?

Michelle Kooi: People can doubt themselves whether they're looking at social media or they're getting feedback from friends or family members about what they should do. I hear people use that word should all the time, and I say, "Don't 'should' on yourself because going forward with intention or with what you want rather than what you should comes with a different energy." It really does. Listen to yourself. That can be getting quiet. I'm a big fan of meditation, but not everybody meditates. We're so busy. We get up and we just go, go, go all day until the time we go to bed. There's no time to think, no time to process, no time to be quiet. Quiet is where ideas can come in. That's where our emotions can come up. We store things in our bodies, so being connected with your body also can help you. There's wisdom there that we can tap into when we get still.

John Creekmur: Recently, Stacy and I have been talking a lot about the way in which we think and that we don't take time as a society to sit down and empty our minds and say, "Let's just be in the moment."

Michelle Kooi: Journaling is another way to brain-dump things out of our heads as well.

John Creekmur: When you're working with people and you walk them through this entire conversation and coaching, where do you start that conversation? Is it with the values conversation? Is it in figuring out who you are as an individual and where you want to go? Or is it the numbers? Where do you find the best place to start that conversation?

Michelle Kooi: I start where they are, so it's not always the same. But I would say if you had to choose between the numbers and the values, it's definitely the values first. Often, especially if I have a client coming to me in a place of scarcity or fear or worry related to finances or money, jumping right into the hard budgeting only brings up more stress. We first need to sit down and understand what's going on. How are you feeling? How did you get here, where did you want to be and where's the gap? What is the impact of what's happening now to you, to your family, to your health, to your retirement, to everything? If you own a business, we need to have a vision and a mission statement. I want to know what that is. If they don't have one, we'll work on that. There are foundations that need to happen before we can get into the technical pieces.

John Creekmur: That's an amazing process, especially for our readers who come from diverse backgrounds. But sometimes, I've noticed that life gets in the way. The pandemic was a prime example. Everyone has different views on that season of time. Some people came out of that period of time with an increased level of anxiety, and their burnout in life and business went up. Have you seen a similar phenomenon with the people you work with? How can you help people reset the conversation and get to a better spot in their business lives and personal lives as it relates to burnout?

Michelle Kooi: I can talk all day about this topic because I personally experienced it several times, to a point of having a serious health impact for myself. I know what it feels like. It creeps up on you. During the pandemic, there were so many different aspects going on. But health is one of my values, so I love bringing that into the picture and connecting clients to that. During the pandemic, connection was lost. We were shut down for a while, and we weren't able to hug people. When we were able to get back together, you had to keep your distance. Human connection was disintegrated for a while, but I feel that created a sense of loneliness, which I find is still a thread that's out there in the world.

We're helping people build back to what's important. From my perspective, if your health is compromised by stress or anxiety, it's hard to be fully present in any place in your life. It's hard to be your best at work, with your kids, with your spouse or with your friends when you are exhausted. We dive into that and help with tools to address that. Many of my clients are also in mental health therapy for anxiety, but some are not. There are different tools we can use that can help calm the nervous system. That's one thing I love about yoga and meditation; it does calm the nervous system, but there are other tools we can use. I believe in food as medicine, so I'll even dive into that as well. I have a certification in holistic health coaching as well.

John Creekmur: It's amazing how it's all connected. We're always in different places with transition or change in our lives. You've been through a couple of transitions professionally, going from the CPA world to starting your own consulting coaching business. When you walk through transitions, how does your approach help clients embrace the expected or even the unexpected aspects of change?

Michelle Kooi: Change and transition can be scary because there's an unknown factor to it. There's an uncertainty, and when there's an uncertainty, we feel out of control, and that brings up anxiety. It's a big loop. But we can't know what's going to happen next. We don't know when our last day is. Life can change in an instant.

How do we want to live each day so that it is most fulfilling and uses our best gifts? We're not going to be experts in everything. I tell my business clients, "You didn't go into graphic design to become an expert in taxes and accounting." Surrounding yourself with people who know things you don't is important. More information can help reduce that anxiety and prepare you for uncertainty, so planning for different scenarios can also help with that.

I also talk to them about how they want to feel through that process. Somebody is going to be changing jobs or starting a business or selling a business, or their youngest child is going off to college. That is a big transition. What do you want to create next in that phase? There are a lot of unknowns, but how do you want to feel? What's important to bring up? What's next? Again, how do you feel? We're not just creating an outline and designing everything, but we're asking how you want it to feel as well so there's an ease and a flow and a joy to it. It's not so hard.

John Creekmur: I can imagine your clients are coming from varied backgrounds. They have a lot of different things happening in life, and sometimes they're navigating those things individually. If they're married or they're in relationships, they're navigating through with another partner in some way. Do you think there is a point when it's best to bring the other individual into the conversation?

Michelle Kooi: Absolutely. I was just thinking about this a bit earlier. I have done some couples' financial coaching, and communication is so important. There's usually one partner in the relationship who is maybe doing more of the balancing the checkbook or paying the bills. But that doesn't mean the other spouse needs to be completely extricated and have no idea what's going on. They need to be involved too. It's a unit.

One of the biggest reasons for divorce is arguments over finances. I think it's hugely important that couples discuss and really know what is going on many different levels and are in agreement. If there's disagreement, they need to be comfortable talking about it. Avoidance can be a big thing that comes into play with couples and money. Shame is also something I have seen come up with clients related to money. They have different spending habits. How were they brought up? How was money talked about when they were growing up? How was money dealt with in their families? That can really shine a light on how they're dealing with things now, and they can make a different choice if that's not how they want to be.

John Creekmur: We all have different backgrounds we bring into relationships. A married couple may go through pre-marital counseling, but they think, "We're in love. We're not going to have those issues." Then, they're married and they think, "Why are we butting heads so much? Why are we not seeing things eye to eye?" We need to recognize the uniqueness of each individual in a relationship and recognize that we all have different backgrounds. If we're not careful, we can actually use those experiences to shame or to manipulate, and that is not at all what we should be doing. Working with someone on that is so critically important.

When I was thinking about coaching, I was thinking about the different personal values individuals have. We're talking about couples. Do you think it's best to walk through the same practice with couples to identify core values as you would with individuals, or do you think it's a bit different?

Michelle Kooi: It's a bit different. I think it is important to identify that with couples, but most likely they're not going to have the exact same values. There definitely may be some crossover. Maybe they have one or two of the same five core values, but it'd be unlikely that all five align. I suppose it's possible, but I think that also helps them understand each other and what's important to them in their lives. We're all individuals, and that helps them be able to support each other's goals and desires and interests.

John Creekmur: You talk about the five core principles people need to focus on in order to live incredible lives. You need to know your core values, set goals based upon your core values, be open to wise counsel, set financial resources to realize goals and value your health. I was just chuckling to myself thinking I've never shared those with you, and yet for last 30 minutes, we have walked through all five of those. I think it's uniquely amazing.

Michelle Kooi: There's alignment.

John Creekmur: Let's say you could spend 15 minutes sitting down and talking with anybody, alive or passed away. Who would that be for you and why?

Michelle Kooi: For me, I think that would be Oprah Winfrey. I respect her, and I'm so impressed by what she's created. Her curiosity for learning and making change herself is really inspiring.

Michelle Kooi, CPA, CPCC/ACC became a Life and Business Coach to help women like her get the support, guidance, reflection, self-care and confidence they need to reach their goals without burning out and to live and work feeling more aligned and empowered.

Michelle supports smart, overwhelmed women in business to feel like themselves again so they are energized and can spend more time on what they want and less time on what they don't. With twenty years of experience working with small businesses as a CPA, she now balances her coaching business and a life full of adventure instead of tax returns. Michelle especially enjoys working with women with ADHD, diagnosed or undiagnosed.

web | www.confluencecoaching.life
email | mkooicc@confluencecoaching.life

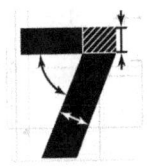

NATALIE PERRY, J.D., CPA

Legacy Matters: Exploring Estate Planning

YOUR BLUEPRINT FOR PURPOSE

YOU HAVE WORKED TIRELESSLY, you are driven to accomplish great things, your focus has been built on a passion to live an incredible life, to be the best that not only you can be, but also a person of impact for generations.

Often times the difference between being where you are and getting to where you want to be is razor thin. It may seem so thin, like a couple sheets of paper. In reality, I have seen the difference between an aspirational life and a fulfilled life is truly an actual couple sheet of paper.

Estate Planner and Trust Administrator Natalie Perry has encountered this situation many times before. These often sad circumstances could have had a much greater impact if they had been aligned more closely with core values, simply by applying a couple of sheets of paper correctly after a meaningful discussion filled with deep questions.

After this conversation, my wife Stacy and I started to revisit our own journey and began another deeper discussion. As you read, begin to ask yourself big question.

SCAN ME TO LISTEN TO NATALIE'S FULL INTERVIEW

NATALIE PERRY, J.D., CPA

John Creekmur: Natalie, would you take some time to introduce yourself, your background and where you're situated right now?

Natalie Perry: I am a practicing attorney in the estate planning field, and I started my career back in the late eighties with Arthur Anderson doing tax planning and tax structuring for clients. But I ended up leaving to go to law school, which I really enjoyed. I've been practicing law for about 25 years. I enjoy the practice I'm in. It's great to be able to work with the families and the people. You really feel like you're making an impact on someone's life at a difficult time when you're dealing with the administration of an estate or even just helping them tie everything together. That way, when something does happen, they can feel a little bit more prepared and try to minimize some of the stress of that time.

John Creekmur: When should a person begin looking through their estate planning? Is it whenever their spouse has passed away or is it many years in advance?

Natalie Perry: Ideally, we would say many years in advance because when your spouse passes away, you want to make sure your spouse had an estate plan depending on your family situation. If you're married, no kids, everything's maybe joint, depending. Now, this is disregarding taxes of course, but perhaps in that situation, your joint assets are going to flow right to your spouse, no issue. But that is rarely the case. We see much more complicated situations: kids from second marriages, assets titled with a beneficiary. There are so many things that can end up not being as simple as people expected. Having a conversation ahead of time can give people peace of mind when they dig into some of those questions.

John Creekmur: Can you identify some of those things people need to be aware of in second marriages, either from the first spouse having passed away or they walk through a divorce situation? Can you walk through some of the pitfalls people don't think about how that affect their estate planning moving forward?

Natalie Perry: It's important to think about those relationships and how your passing away will affect your kids and your spouse. For example, maybe you've got kids that don't get along with your second wife or second husband depending on the situation. Typically, you might name your spouse as your executor or trustee of your estate plan, but if that's going to create a problem because they don't like each other, you might want to rethink that. Maybe a bank makes sense. You could go with a trusted advisor like an accountant or an attorney, somebody a bit more neutral to let you get assets transferred and administered without pulling teeth. That, I'd say, is the biggest issue we try to avoid: this friction or this difficulty in that relationship.

Another issue is deciding who should get what, because maybe your spouse does need the rest of your money for the rest of his or her lifetime. That's an important feature. Maybe some should be in a trust so that when your spouse dies, some of it goes to your kids from the first marriage. There are a lot of ways to set that up. That's something you should talk about with your advisor.

John Creekmur: I had a couple as clients who were on their second marriage and whose previous spouses had both passed away from cancer. But they both came in with their own children, and then they had children together. Whenever the husband passed away, everything was titled to the wife, and when she passed away, all of his money was passed on to his second wife's children. The families ended up working together for a good solution. But often, we don't see that.

Natalie Perry: You hate to see them fighting or spending a lot of money on legal fees over who should have gotten what. It sounds like your situation ended up with a great result, which is good.

John Creekmur: But it doesn't always work that way. That's why you want to make sure you actually have these discussions ahead of time. I had a client last week who was getting ready to head into retirement. He was at the executive level. He was asking, "Now that I'm heading to a new life stage, when should I go through reviewing my estate plan?" Do you think heading into retirement would be a good time to review your estate plans?

Natalie Perry: Yes, I think that is a good time to review your plan. Probably for the most significant reason is you'll have a little more time to devote to it. I think that is a great time to rethink where you are going to live. Maybe you're going to move to Florida or take up residency in another state, even if it's part-time. That may be something that changes your estate plan. Maybe your assets have grown significantly since the last time you looked at your estate plan, and that would cause you to want to update some things. Then, like you said, maybe you're closer to one child than the other, or your one child is nearby, and they ought to be tasked with some of the administrative items in your estate plan. Maybe you had named somebody else before. All those things make it important to review.

We do sometimes get clients who come in and say, "I want to update my estate plan," and we look at it, and we don't need to change anything. But keeping on top of those decisions and refreshing your memory about whom you named, and why, is always a good exercise to go through as it really helps keep things fresh.

John Creekmur: You have both a CPA and your law degree. Do you see a real benefit in having both of those backgrounds when you're walking through estate planning issues?

Natalie Perry: Yes, I do. I tend to work with a fair amount of business owners, and that's partly because I have the accounting background and the tax planning background, so I have a good understanding of financial documents. I also spent some years at JP Morgan, so I learned a fair amount about investing and the types of accounts out there, and that has also been a real benefit. But I think having that background is very helpful to be able to advise clients on all these issues, because it is such a big-picture practice area. It's not just about who gets what; it's, what are the tax implications? If I leave money to my kids in trust, what are the tax implications of that? What are the income tax implications of having money in a trust? Thinking through all those issues is very important and helpful to clients.

John Creekmur: Many people think they don't really need to do estate planning because they're not billionaires. From an estate tax standpoint, are there certain thresholds where all of a sudden, we have estate tax issues? Below that threshold, is estate planning still beneficial?

Natalie Perry: Tax is one, and I think probate avoidance is sometimes an issue as well. Then planning for minor children. But let's start back with the tax concept. Here in Illinois, we do have a state estate tax that taxes assets. Once you've hit $4 million of assets, they tax all of your assets. That is a much lower exemption than the federal exemption, which is currently $13,610,000 per person, so it's really very high. Under the Trump Tax Act from 2017, that amount is set to revert in 2026, and if they don't do anything, it's automatically going to go back to $5 million, but indexed for inflation, so we think it might end up at $6 million or $7 million per person. That is a pretty significant change that clients are already starting to think about and wonder what they should be doing, if anything. That's obviously going to affect the clients with a little bit more wealth who may be in a position to give some away or do some additional planning.

We've got the estate tax, and then we've got the probate avoidance. A lot of people don't like their assets to become public record or to have their wills filed with the county where they reside. Sometimes, we end up doing a trust which can avoid that and keep some of those things more private.

John Creekmur: You've mentioned that in 2026, we're reverting back to what the tax law was before the 2017 tax code change as it relates to estate planning and income tax planning. We have this window of opportunity over the next year and a half to start working through some estate planning and income tax planning decisions. How far in advance do you think it's wise for a person to start that process, knowing that we have this window starting to close a bit?

Natalie Perry: I think lawyers and advisors like yourself are going to be quite busy having these conversations over the next year and a half, and the sooner the better, even if they don't pull the trigger. Be aware of the issues and understand what might make sense for your family, whether it is some sort of gift trust or a straight gift to your adult children, if you've got them. Thinking about that ahead of time is wise. My guess is a lot of estate planners are going to be quite busy next year figuring out solutions for clients. The banks will have to open up new accounts or get tax ID numbers. All of that also takes time.

John Creekmur: So many people wait until April 15th to think about things. We're a country of procrastinators. I would encourage everyone to spend some time thinking about estate planning topics before they actually get to the end of the year in 2025.

We briefly touched on charitable giving. What does charitable giving look like within someone's estate plan?

Natalie Perry: It runs the gamut of types of techniques depending on the client's intentions. You may see, on the higher side, somebody starting a private foundation, and those are not as popular as they used to be with the onset of the donor-advised fund. We see a lot of people putting money into donor-advised funds, which are accounts at financial institutions or charitable institutions where that money can sit and then be doled out over time. A private foundation is for the client who has a little bit more to give and is able to set up more of an ongoing, business-like entity put in place for the purpose of making charitable gifts or grants for a certain charitable purpose or multiple purposes. Those can be great for families who want to leave a legacy or get their kids involved in their charitable giving.

Then, we might see straight gifts, gifts to my church, gifts to my alma mater, my favorite local charity, whatever that may be, or a bigger national charity given some of the disasters we've seen happening. In between, there are some trusts that allow for a gift to charity over a limited time period, say 10 years. There are trusts for charity that can terminate at a person's death, and then the balance goes to children. There's a lot of creativity involved in charitable giving depending on the client's interest and desire, how they want to give it and what the numbers look like.

John Creekmur: You mentioned the donor-advised fund. It's interesting that in the last five to seven years we have seen so many clients in a lot of different spots from a socio-economic standpoint utilize the donor-advised fund as one of their charitable giving tools. It has been a phenomenal way for people to build up some legacy even in their families as they donate some highly appreciated assets or receive higher deductions as far as the current year, but then a couple have actually set up what they would call family boards. It's not an official board, but they have a family meeting and each child and grandchild has to present a charity that's near and dear to them. Then, they have to do research and present it, and the whole family then votes on what's going to be given to and what's not. It's been a way to teach legacy topic to that next generation instead of just the actual dollar amount. I love that thought and that concept.

Natalie Perry: Those are really great and much simpler for clients to manage. There's not so much administration.

John Creekmur: For sure. People are living longer now, which is really a great blessing. But that means that our family dynamics are actually growing and expanding. We have children and then grandchildren and sometimes great-grandchildren. Sometimes, we have families that are growing through adoption. How does all of that change impact a client's estate planning? Are those things that they need to be considering regularly?

Natalie Perry: I think that's very client-specific, because some clients do like the idea of a dynasty trust, where they can put some money aside and have it grow over generations. It's exempt from tax and it can sit there and accumulate and serve multiple generations or pay for college for these kids and grandkids that they might not even meet or know. Other clients just want their money to go to their children outright. They'll say, "I don't want a trust. That's so complicated. That's only for rich people."

But it really depends. If you're comfortable with a trust, there is a lot of impact to be made for future generations, and it doesn't have to be $20 million; it can be a few million or $5 million. There's no limit on what is given, so it is a very powerful tool as we are living longer. That ties into our earlier conversation about the exemption going down. People may want to start thinking about whether they should set aside money in some sort of trust that could go on for generations.

John Creekmur: You did mention that you work with a lot of small business owners, and I know the definition of a small business owner changes depending on where people are at and how their businesses have grown over the years. Can you walk through pitfalls they may not see and also opportunities they might not consider?

Natalie Perry: That's a great question. There are some additional issues I always tell my clients to think about when they do have operating businesses. The first one goes back to that control point I've made a few times. If you have an ongoing business and when you die, you anticipate that business will continue to exist, what should happen to it? Who should be in charge of it? It could be that your spouse is the best person. Perhaps they've been very involved, and they're familiar with your accounts and your customers and how the business is run. But then there are probably other situations where the spouse isn't the right person. Maybe they were raising the kids or they had their own profession of some sort. In that case, you may need to look for another advisor or perhaps an employee or manager at the company who can step in and help with those business decisions once the owner isn't alive to make them.

That's where we see some plans go awry or some disputes come up: when there isn't someone named with the capability and skill to make the decisions. We can end up selling the business for less than anticipated, or there could be an abrupt shutdown if customers decide this isn't the same business as it was. That is a really big point. A buy-sell agreement often can make sense, or the right of first refusal might be built into a shareholders' agreement if you have an LLC. If you have partners or investors, you must know their expectations in case something happens to them. Should that person have the right to buy out your shares first and then your spouse ends up with the cash?

Similarly, should you be able to buy that person out if something happens to them in order to have continuity in the business? There, we might want to look at life insurance or some sort of valuation mechanism. How are we going to value that business? We probably don't want to use book value, but fair-market value with an appraisal might not be the right number either. We have to come to an agreement and really dig into what's going to work for all the parties involved.

Those are probably the two biggest things I see, but there can be others with real estate. Perhaps the business is sitting on some real estate. Is there a lease? Should that real estate be separated out? Is it okay for the kids to get that? There's really a lot to think about.

John Creekmur: There are so many details to think through, so make sure to work with an attorney that has the background and the knowledge to say, "Hey, consider these things."

I've had a number of clients who've done extremely well either owning a small business or as executives of large companies, and one of the questions they're asking is, "We have accumulated a large amount of net worth. How much is appropriate to leave to our children and grandchildren?" It always comes back to, "That's a personal question." Is there a professional way to view that?

Natalie Perry: We see that a lot. A lot of people don't want their kids to just walk into this money they didn't earn. Some people might fix what the kids get; each person gets $5 million, and that's it. The rest goes to charity or some sort of foundation or maybe grandchildren or a trust for grandchildren. But we can do a lot with formulas for clients like that because they can escape tax. If we've fixed the dollar amount that goes to the kids, then we can have the rest be a charitable gift that we've structured to be exempt from estate tax. For somebody with a large amount of wealth who doesn't want the kids to get every dollar, that can be a great way for charity to benefit but also for those kids to get a meaningful amount of money.

Often, if you are over the exemption, the kids aren't going to get that money anyway. It's going to go to taxes, and a lot of people don't like that idea. They don't want the government getting their hard-earned money. Depending on your views, there are definitely options for structuring gifts to children.

You may also want to look at what they're going to get outright. Maybe you have an IRA or a 401k, and those are harder to retain in trust for a longer time period. If they're going to get some sort of seed money from these retirement accounts, maybe the rest of the wealth they get should be kept in a more restrictive trust that they can access eventually.

What's the right age? Is it 50? Is it 60? Is it when some things happen in their lives where you feel like they might be ready to handle some of that money? You can really be creative in a trust and work with the client to get deep on what they care about but not in a heavy-handed way.

John Creekmur: I love the concept of the formula. I think that does take into consideration the estate tax issues and also helps give some framework for the family to walk through those decisions. That's an excellent recommendation. Natalie, you're based in Chicagoland. But let's say somebody is searching from LA or Texas or Florida, and they're looking to work with an estate planning attorney. How do they decide whom to work with?

Natalie Perry: Obviously, you want to look at the credentials and ideally work with a specialist. It depends on your market. You might not be able to find somebody who does the estate planning day-in and day-out, but those are really the people that are going to have the deep expertise that I have. That's all we're doing every day: talking to clients about who gets what, the tax implications, the family issues. You can look at the person's background for sure.

There's also a group called ACTEC, which is the American College of Trusts and Estate Council. Their website is www.actec.org. I'm part of ACTEC. It's made up of peer-nominated estate planning attorneys all over the United States who are recommended by their colleagues in their local markets. That might be one place to look if you're in a region where you don't have a local contact who can help you. You could look on their website and search by your state.

John Creekmur: That's a great resource. Natalie, we've covered a lot of information over the last 30 minutes. Is there anything we've not covered that you really think readers should be aware of concerning tax and estate planning?

Natalie Perry: A big misconception we didn't get to talk much about, is that lot of people think they don't need an estate plan either because they don't have enough money or because they want everything to go to their wives and kids. Often, that's not the case under state law. If you're married with two children, even if they're minors, state law often says that the assets go half to the spouse and half to the kids. That could create some real complications for people who may not have awareness. You could get a very simple will online or with a lawyer. Lawyers are always better in my opinion. People don't always realize that's how things work, and when we go back to that second-marriage scenario, that could definitely be a concern, or maybe you've got kids from multiple marriages. Just having a basic estate plan is more important than people think. I'm not saying that everyone will hire a lawyer. It can just be so much easier and less expensive to have the planning done up front.

Natalie M. Perry, J.D., CPA is a partner at Harrison LLP with over two decades of experience in tax-efficient estate planning and income tax planning.

She is a registered Certified Public Accountant (CPA) and an attorney with expertise in high-net-worth estate planning, trust disputes resolution and probate administration.

Natalie has also worked as a tax consultant for closely held businesses and is a frequent speaker at professional education events. Additionally, she has been recognized for contributions to the estate planning community and is involved in various professional organizations.

web | www.harrisonllp.com
email | nperry@harrisonllp.com
phone | (312) 753 - 6160
office | 333 W. Wacker Drive, Suite 1700
Chicago, IL 60606

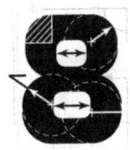

BABS PLUNKETT

How to Find Joy in Life as an Empty Nester

YOUR BLUEPRINT FOR PURPOSE

A LL I CAN SAY ABOUT BABS, IS JOY. Really... Joy. The passion to pursue Joy in each step and the next step is critical. So many people get to the next stage of their life- also referred to as retirement- and they run out of Joy. It is so strange that most people spend the first 60 yrs of their life working, saving, sacrificing to get to retirement, and then they live a life devoid of JOY.

Finding meaning, staying healthy, developing relationships, these do not happen just out of happenchance, they are intentional. They are part of the formula to find Joy and to live a Joy-filled life.

Taking certain steps can derail where you are going. We can get distracted and become the deer in the headlights, frozen and unable to act. That is why Babs uses practical wisdom to spread Joy to thousands of people.

Share in that Joy with Babs.

SCAN ME TO LISTEN TO BAB'S FULL INTERVIEW

John Creekmur: Babs Plunkett is a Certified Retirement Coach and Life Coach and the bestselling author of *Choose Joy: Three keys to Investing Your Time in Retirement*. Babs, can you tell us a bit about your background?

Babs Plunkett: I help people empty-nest through retirement rediscover their purpose.

In general, we typically get our purpose from our paid work or from the defined roles in society, such as being a parent. When we retire from fulltime work and from fulltime parenthood, we lose the structure of our days, the definition of our role in the world, the sense of purpose that comes from that role and often the friends that go with it. As parents, we need to make the transition to treating our adult kids like the adults they are, instead of clinging to them for our purpose.

Parents who still rely on their kids for a sense of purpose may feel stuck at best or create tension with their kids at worst. That can look like relying on grandkids to fill the purpose gap, which puts pressure on the young adult kids to fulfill our need for meaning.

John Creekmur: Do you find that most people struggle in that transition initially, or is that something which they grow through in time?

Babs Plunkett: When I started doing this work, I thought I was going to work exclusively with people in retirement. I was very surprised to discover that people early in the retirement phase, both women and men, talked about their purpose as still connected with their children. It was surprising to me to see how much those are interrelated and how often in our culture we define ourselves by what we do. The two things we spend the most time doing are our paid work and our roles as parents. Once the kids are gone, it's caring for aging parents. Those roles are how we define ourselves, and when those jobs are done, who are we?

John Creekmur: My wife and I have three boys. They're 30, 27 and 24. Stacy and I are empty-nesters now, so we're trying to get used to managing our time. We were the parents of three boys. Our life was so wrapped up in raising them and then releasing them into young adulthood. Now, who are we as individuals? I know you probably have seen lots of sad stories of people who have struggled in that race. But it seems to be all-encompassing. It relates to our health, our mobility and the things that we do, our joy or lack of joy. Do you see this journey as a focus on one area, or is it more of a holistic approach?

Babs Plunkett: It's a holistic approach. It's helpful for people to address this empty-nest phase before the retirement phase. We're fairly clear about retirement. We know we are no longer going to show up at work 40, 50, 60 hours a week. That's a lot of free time to plan for. Special trips and golfing a couple times each week will not consume 40 hours each week.

But as I mentioned earlier, the first thing we retire from is full-time parenthood. If you had three boys, you were probably on a ton of sports and extracurricular sidelines. The friends you hung out with were probably the parents of your boys' friends. The first thing we retire from is that role as parents, so we lose the structure of our after-work hours or our weekends. Those tournaments are done. We lose a lot of the connections that we had, so we lose some friendships, and we lose one of the ways that we define ourselves.

The same thing is true with retiring from paid work. We lose the structure of our day, we lose the definition of our role in the world, and we usually lose the connections that went with that. We do not talk about this loss. We've worked with these people for 30 years, and we think we're going to stay in touch. Maybe that will happen, but sadly for most people, work friends don't continue. The struggles in the empty-nest are similar to the struggles in retirement. It's just an iterative wave of transitions.

John Creekmur: I'm sure it applies to some of those practical things as far as our daily schedules go. But do you find it also applies to a level of joy or contentment or meaning?

Babs Plunkett: Absolutely, yes. In both our paid work and our roles as parents, what it means to be a "good" worker/parent are quite prescribed. Maybe they're unconscious, but you wouldn't have to think very long to define what society says equals a good dad, a good mom, a good worker. The way you spend your time determines whether you're a good parent. Maybe you coached; that's a good parent. It defines how you invest your time, and it brings you tons of joy. Nothing probably brought you more joy than the time you spent with your boys. For decades, you were investing your time outside of your work in these human beings. Then, they leave, and you have 20 extra hours a week to redefine how you want to invest that time outside of your paid work.

How you invest your time meaningfully is yet another wave of questions. When we're doing the parent thing, it's satisfying. As a parent, you're happy to give all those decades of time. The people I work with are smart and competent. They get stuff done in every other area of their lives, so they feel really confused and frustrated that they can't figure out what they like to do outside of their roles as parents or paid workers. Lots of people don't know this because they've invested their time in other things for decades. They paused their hobbies, volunteering, and time with friends.

John Creekmur: Is it a challenge to figure that out?

Babs Plunkett: For some, it's a shorter struggle if they happen to have kept hobbies going or have longed for something and they can say, "Finally, I can learn to play the guitar."

But for many people it is a struggle. This is especially true for really high achievers, who have dedicated their lives to their work. They are often surprised by how challenging it is, and feel kind of embarrassed that they can't think of anything that they like to do just for themselves. They think, "What's the matter with me? Why can't I think of what I love?"

John Creekmur: What was the inspiration behind your book *Choose Joy: Three Keys to Investing Your Time in Retirement*? I know it has a lot of great stories. Was hearing those stories what prompted you to write that book?

Babs Plunkett: I first got interested in how to age well when I was 13. That's when my grandma moved in with my family and she was the crabbiest person I'd ever met! As a young person, I thought, "Am I genetically programmed to grow up like her?" Her crabbiness inspired me to start asking people who seemed to be happy adults this question: "Were you born this way, or did you make up your mind to be happy?" The first person I asked was my seventh-grade teacher, Mr. McMullen. He was the first of hundreds of people to say, "Oh, no I wasn't born this way. I had to focus on choosing to be positive." They could name when they made up their minds to live with intention. They made up their minds to choose joy.

I did my honors thesis in college on this and continued to chat informally with happy people over the decades. Then when my mom was at the end of her life, she was as crabby as her mom, although she'd said, "Girls, you tell me if I'm ever like her." I felt it imperative to figure this out. I couldn't just count on my good attitude right now as a relatively young person. So I started interviewing people. I cast a wide net, asking my social network to connect me to older adults who are aging with joy and purpose. It was so much fun to interview these incredible people.

John Creekmur: Were there any common characteristics you saw in those stories?

Babs Plunkett: Yes. One common thing was they universally dispelled a myth about finding purpose in retirement. I think a lot of people get bogged down by a belief that you leave your paid work or parenting and need to find this giant thing. We think of purpose as this one, big, singular thing. Instead, the people I interviewed described their new purpose as an intentional collection of choices that align with their values. The majority of those living with joy also ensured that in a typical day, typical week, typical month, they have three things going on.

First, they have something to engage their minds with a sense of purpose. It can be a variety of things ranging from volunteering, a creative pursuit, or active learning. But they all scheduled things that really matter to them and make an impact.

Second, they're committed to moving the body. 20 minutes a day is enough to bring significant health benefits.

Third is connecting with others. Loneliness is an epidemic. It was an epidemic before our pandemic, and the Harvard study on adult development discovered that loneliness kills at the same rate as smoking and alcoholism.

John Creekmur: That is staggering.

Babs Plunkett: Yes, it is. Even a connection with one person can have health benefits, can decrease Alzheimer's and the risk of heart attack. It's profound. I help my clients get reconnected with others and with themselves. We explore, what are their skills outside of their work? What are they passionate about? What do they really care about? Then, we create a collection of intentional choices that align with those values and put it on their calendar, so you don't have to rely on a good night's sleep or a good attitude. It's built into how you live.

John Creekmur: You outlined three keys here, and on paper, they seem simple. But do people have hurdles to accomplishing those three things?

Babs Plunkett: Oh my goodness, there are so many. Take loneliness, for instance. There's a self-talk that says, "There's nobody out there. I live too far away from my family. I'm retired now, and my friends are all from work." This is particularly true for men. Men tend to rely on their spouses for their social connection. If the marriage ends—and 50% of marriages do end in that empty-nest phase—they don't have the tools to connect. For women who are mothers, their friends often come from their kids' lives, and it's a shock when their kids leave. You've got to start over, and that can be difficult.

John Creekmur: I know you have put together a number of incredible classes and other resources. How can people interact with those? Is it as simple as getting your book and reading it, or is it better for them to walk through a class or engage in some other way?

Babs Plunkett: For a highly self-motivated person, starting with my book, *Choose Joy: Three Keys to Investing Your Time in Retirement* is a great place to get rolling. It's a collection of 50 stories of how wise ones have done it. It's sort of like *Chicken Soup for the Soul*. They're very readable, inspiring stories. After each story there's a "try this" idea. If something inspires you, there's a concrete action you can take. There's a free guidebook that goes along with the book.

If you're someone who would like a bit more support, I have several ways I can help. You can join my free Facebook community, the "Empty Nesters' Joyful Purpose Club" where I post content five days a week and smart women swap ideas on living with joy.

YOUR BLUEPRINT FOR PURPOSE

If you know that you achieve better with some direct support or you're not even sure how to begin, I offer private coaching where I create a personalized plan for finding your purpose.

Don't waste a couple of years struggling to figure this out alone.

A jarring wake-up for me when I entered the empty-nest phase was realizing I still had 35 years of living. I wasn't going to waste it. Life is too short.

John Creekmur: It truly is, and we're all managers of the time we've been given. You mentioned materials for women, but do you have a specific class for women?

Babs Plunkett: Yes, I do have a course that's exclusively for women called the "Choose Joy Method to Rediscover Your Purpose" that provides a step-by-step plan, nurturing accountability and the support of a welcoming group of smart women working to uncover their unique skills/gifts/values/passions that lead to a new plan for purpose. I created it because many women prefer to process in a group.

I find men tend to prefer one-on-one coaching. In private coaching I guide people through the same core concepts: What are your values? What are your skills outside of your paid work or skills that you want to carry forward from your paid work to the next phase of life? What do you care about? What are your passions? We create a plan to invest your time on a typical day, week and month.

I help people align their daily choices with the things they care about. It sounds basic, but it takes some work. For both men and women, we tend to carry with us some limiting beliefs, a little bit of baggage, which I help people release. For women, there can be people-pleasing habits that hold us back. Our worth is based on making other people happy. For men, their worth often comes from being a good provider, so when the job of provider is done, what is your worth? We discover many other ways you can give your good to the world.

John Creekmur: How does active listening play into walking through this journey of joy? Do people need to be active listeners to process things well?

Babs Plunkett: Active listening is core to how I support people. With that active, deep listening, I help them hear their own wisdom. I hear it both from men and women who really need help sorting their thoughts and getting clear on how they want to use their precious time. An example of active listing is with an attorney I'm working with right now who is not used to sharing his thoughts and his feelings. He marvels that this is possible, that he can learn to process out loud and in written form. He is finding it revelatory to get reconnected with what he cares about. How does he want to live? What matters to him? That comes from deep, active listening.

John Creekmur: That's amazing. Now Babs, would someone looking to use your services need to be geographically close to you, or can you work remotely?

Babs Plunkett: All my clients are remote. I've had clients from Nova Scotia to British Columbia to Southern Florida to California and everywhere in between. I've even connected with people in India and Romania. By using Zoom or cell phones, anything is possible today.

John Creekmur: When people are trying to create plans to walk through this transition, is there some general advice they need to be thinking about or some preliminary ideas they need to be chewing on?

Babs Plunkett: I would bring it back to the three keys I offer in my book.

1. Engage Your Mind: Choose at least one activity to engage your mind with a sense of meaning outside of your paid work. It really makes a difference to begin two or three years before you retire so you're not retiring from something but rather into something.

Choose something to engage your mind. Get aligned with what you care about and find a way to engage your mind with a sense of purpose, something you can do weekly.

2. Move Your Body: Move in any way for a minimum of 20 minutes every day. It can be anything: gardening, walking, pickleball.

3. Connect with Others: Do the work to create relationships with other people. Research shows even one connection can make a difference. Sometimes, you can combine them. A simple way to get those going is to do what I call a walk and talk. Put in your earbuds and connect with a friend anywhere in the world.

Set a phone date and go for a walk. I have a friend who lives 2,000 miles away, and we walk every Monday. I have a brother who lives 1,000 miles away; we have a standing phone date twice a month. There are ways to bridge the loneliness outside of geography. Technology makes anything possible.

Babs Plunkett a Certified Retirement Coach and Life Coach and the bestselling author of *Choose Joy: Three Keys to Investing Your Time in Retirement.*

Babs is also the founder of the *Choose Joy Method to Rediscover Your Purpose* online course and host of the free Facebook group "Empty Nesters' Joyful Purpose Club," a fun place to make new friends and swap ideas on living fully in this next phase of life.

web | www.babsplunkett.com
email | babs@babsplunkett.com

NANCY SCHWARTZ

Transform Health into Retirement Wealth

YOUR BLUEPRINT FOR PURPOSE

DOES THIS SOUND FAMILIAR: "I was an exhausted and frustrated corporate consultant. I struggled with sustained energy and declining health, despite being a health nut. Working in a high stress environment, I found myself compelled to find a solution to this unsustainable lifestyle. I knew that moving forward, I would have to work to intentionally carve out a life that I wanted to live. As I neared retirement, I began to consider my next steps."

All I know is that Nancy's journey is a summary of most everyone that we encounter daily in our conversations. It probably sounds a little like your own journey.

When you are working to live an incredible life, you have embraced your core values, you are overcoming hurdles, you are working diligently to save and accumulate, and put into place the proper documents to execute, it can all become overwhelming, without Joy.

Nancy shares lessons learned through her own personal journey of how to execute the next stage.

SCAN ME TO LISTEN TO NANCY'S FULL INTERVIEW

John Creekmur: Nancy, can you give us a quick overview of your personal journey, your background, and what you do right now?

Nancy Schwartz: Very simply, I was *that* corporate executive. I worked for 40 years very diligently in retained executive search. It was very stressful, but we did a lot of great work putting in amazing executives who really changed the course of the business. That often was our directive. I felt very privileged to work within the Global Fortune companies down to private equity, including VC. I spanned a big breadth of industries and categories such as function-specific and the C suite. I did a lot of CFOs, a lot of board work, et cetera. That was really fun, and then I decided I wanted to break all the rules again and built my own company, which was very successful, called SearchExecution. I adored my clients and my candidates, and I felt very privileged to have more freedom than at a public company.

Korn Ferry is the number-one retained executive search firm in the world, and I felt very honored to work in those hallowed halls. I was working late at night, and I said, "I think it's getting time to retire, but what should I be doing? I don't know. How do I get off this hamster wheel?" I was so used to it. Our thought process becomes so automatic. This was a five-year journey to learning much more about retirement from the physical, the social and the emotional point of view.

I also felt I needed health support. How can I change my life so that I can disrupt the way we think about retirement today? Because it doesn't exist. We have the privilege today to make up our own retirement journey. Everyone does. But you can't have retirement without your health. What's so exciting is the science and technology is changing radically. What can we do today to promote our health so that it will impact our longevity?

We know the statistics are very forbearing in terms of illness and also in terms of situations we could either catch early or that we simply can fly over. The wellness industry is massive, but we make sure that it's really anchored in the science and the knowledge and to keep upgrading that to help those we serve. That's what I do. I work with business experts in and around retirement to set them on a path toward longevity and freedom and to do what they want to do.

John Creekmur: When working with executives and folks preparing for this stage, I don't like the word retirement. We just call it the next stage of life. We all know what retirement is, and it's about heading to that next stage of life. When it comes to entering that stage, have you found that what people envision is actually different from reality?

Nancy Schwartz: Yes, a hundred percent. I come at this in a couple of different ways. We go to school, be it college or trade school, working to build this skill set. Then, we then go to work, and we progress through the companies or we're recruited out. Somehow, we acquire these skill sets. At some point, all of us will retire. And as you say, this word is globally hated. But at that next chapter in life, we can have many retirements. I have had many retirements myself. It's very expansive, and you are only limited by how you think about it, how you design it.

You use the word intention. It's about doing, learning and figuring out your next steps. That is called life. Life doesn't stop. That's what

I think you and I are trying to express to the audience, that life keeps going on. Just because you enter into this stage doesn't mean you don't have problems, and it also doesn't mean you can't keep evolving.

John Creekmur: Yet there is a certain level of planning along the way. I thought I had seen somewhere on one of your websites the phrase, "Plan you, own you, move you." Can you walk through that phase and how you help people transition in those three areas?

Nancy Schwartz: I was starting to see in the marketplace that we don't educate in terms of how to do this in the marketplace. We work with our companies, and we save money. Yes, we will financially invest in portfolios. Yes, our company will match. There's education there if you care to take part in it. But what is lacking in the market is you, the person. Plan for that person; honor yourself. My first biggest takeaway for "Plan You," is to put yourself first. When was the time that you ever put yourself first? I can tell you I was well into my 60s before I ever put myself first. I was brought up to put family first, company first and clients first.

"Own You" means you are 150% responsible for you. Take ownership of yourself so that you can have your authenticity and have agency in life. That's such a big step for people. Your accountant can't help you. Your lawyer can't help you. Your community can lift you up and serve you if you hire these people, but they can't do it for you. You have to take action yourself. This is an interesting concept for people. They don't always take action, but they want things. It requires action.

Lastly, we have "Move You." It is statistically proven that moving your mind, your body and your soul is one of the key elements to overall health. And we don't do it. We just don't do it.

John Creekmur: Right now, our readers are probably saying, "Wait a minute. I thought planning for retirement was solely financial." And I think that the financial services industry has done a huge disservice to people's actual enjoyment and contentment in retirement because all they focus on is the number. We have these green lines, and we've got these orange numbers and all these different things. It revolves around the financial. But you're starting to talk about things that are so much deeper than that, that are much more impactful than that, things like personal well-being and fulfillment. When you start thinking about the different aspects of retirement planning, what do you think is the most impactful part?

Nancy Schwartz: I think it's to honor yourself. It's an opportunity to change your identity, to own the fact that—using myself as an example—I was a corporate executive, but I'm also more than that. That's what I talk about, the expansive piece at the top. You can learn any skillset; it's a matter of putting your heart to it. I continue to educate myself. Every quarter, there's something that I dedicate myself to learning so that I can pass that on. That's the beauty of this business I'm in; I learn something, and it creates impact in me, and then I can share it with my clients. There's an enjoyment. There's a thread that goes through so that my clients can honor themselves.

There's a new book out by Oprah and Arthur Brooks. I've watched a few podcasts, and he's really an extraordinary human, a Harvard professor and just brilliant. He's 59, I believe, and he talks about finding enjoyment at this stage in life, being satisfied with less, but that it serves the purpose, your purpose. You've spoken before about rethinking your value system. Values are made up of a lot of different things. But sometimes we don't update our values for a long time, or we never update them. I also took on some of my company values. We all do, but were they all mine?

In retirement, or this next stage as you call it, you have to live it. It's not something you can imagine. You have to be living and breathing in it. Then, you understand how complex these lifestyles become. You are that living, breathing entity of yourself when you finally step over that line.

John Creekmur: When you're talking about going from this life of doing into a mindset of being, that's a significant change of outlook. It's a change from what we've always known, and we know it's difficult for us to go through change. Often, change brings up fear in people. Have you seen a way or a process for people to start to navigate change and to deal with that fear in the process?

Nancy Schwartz: I'm so passionate about this. You talked about intention. That's a philosophy of your firm, and I love that you share this with your community. So many of us, as you suggested, are living the day-to-day in what I call survival mode. It's a very subconscious living. We just do it. We wake up, we brush our teeth, we go get the train, we go here, we go there. Conscious living is a totally different state of being, and it's very purposeful and driven. There's a wonderful community called the x-change community, and they teach conscious leadership. You have to be a conscious leader to be leading yourself as well. There are so many transferable skill sets from your career into your new operating environment.

That fear factor is huge, and people will procrastinate. They won't take action; they won't move forward. Then what happens? Life passes by. There are a lot of pitfalls in this transition. I'm starting to study some of these very interesting ideas involving our own subconscious in early-stage development. We're learning about this. Through science, we can help eliminate a lot of these limiting belief systems, and fear is part of that. Why am I fearful of this? I always ask people, "What's the origin of that?"

John Creekmur: That's so critical. If we never get past that fear of the unknown because we've been living a life of doing, that has an impact on physical health, mental health and relational health. We are not living life to its fullest extent. You've mentioned science a number of times. How much do you think science plays into this discussion? Is that a large part of what you're finding?

Nancy Schwartz: Yes. For instance, I'm wearing an Oura Ring, wearable technology. There are shirts. There are wristbands. There are a variety of wearables available at the consumer level. I consider myself a consumer. We're going back to ownership. I am owning, "Did I sleep enough last night?" I am owning, "Did I stay up really late and have dinner very late?" There are all sorts of blood-monitoring wearables for diabetes and sugar. The list is endless, and they're not just for elite, CEO-level people that have special teams. This is available to the American consumer now.

John Creekmur: It is so interesting you're bringing this up. The last three years, I've actually become a huge user of different wearables to track pretty much every aspect of my physical being, not just heartbeat but oxygenation, all of my moods and energy levels. It is amazing what we're able to do. I've noticed I've had a higher level of contentment in the projects I'm working on. It has given me a redefined vision of purpose. I think it's interesting how all of that is connected, and I think that as people are transitioning from that period of working and doing into the next phase of life, there are a lot of things they don't know. In the past, their purpose may have been career or family.

In the discussions we have with clients, it always revolves around what is the purpose of what you're doing with this season? What is the purpose of what we're doing? We try to get them to that point. How important would you say is structure and purpose in that next phase? How can somebody create and maintain it after leaving that structured career of what they've always known? Is it more of a journey to develop, or is it more organic?

Nancy Schwartz: We are all driven by the calendar. I don't care if you are the CEO or the parking guy in the garage. You've got to get there at a certain time. If you're the mom who supports the entire family, the hardest job ever, you are driven by the calendar. That's the structure.

I encourage all my clients to put everything in the calendar. In terms of purpose, one of the key drivers to a successful retirement is structure, and that is the synergistic connection between the mind and the heart. That is why that person is living.

But that's for the person. My purpose is to guide executives in and around retirement, and I want to support them on, as you suggested, this journey. But then I want to ask them "Okay, we know your purpose, but what's the impact statement you want?" I believe you can have it in your home. Let's say you're a grandparent. You're caring for the young ones. Or perhaps you're growing a garden or tutoring someone. It could be in your local community. It could be a global endeavor. It can be anything that has purpose and structure.

John Creekmur: I've seen the anecdotal evidence from working with thousands of plot households around the entire world, because the people that actually head to that next phase can clearly state their purposes. We have noticed how they stay on their financial plans, and their variable spending is actually lower because they have a plan and a purpose. They accomplish their financial objectives. On the physical side, I've noticed a higher level of engagement, a higher level of, we'll say relational joy with people, even as they walk into an office or have connection with people. But also from a health standpoint, they don't have a lot of the chronic issues that I see with other folks that cannot name their purposes. They cannot actually describe what their purpose is.

What I've known anecdotally for the last 30 years, you're actually describing from a scientific standpoint. It is huge for people to actually go through and define that, no matter what their stage of lives are in. That is a key component of walking through that next phase successfully.

I've also seen you write about the science of longevity. People are living longer, and there are some fears about a longer life. What does that mean for my time? What does that mean for my financial risk? I have a fear of outliving money, or maybe I have a fear of more health issues the longer I live. It's going to erode my principal balance. When we think about that science of longevity, I know it's a big part of planning at this phase with what you do. What are some key takeaways for living that healthy retirement? What does that look like, and how does that longevity element fit into it?

Nancy Schwartz: Longevity is something relatively new. I love Dr. Peter Attia's statement in his book, *Outlive*, "How are you living in your marginal decades?" When I sought support in financial houses, they said to me, "Well, Nancy, how do you plan year one? What are you going to be doing post-career? Let's look at three years, five years out." But as everyone knows now, we are living 30-40 years longer. Attia's thought is to define the marginal decade as the last decade you are going to be living.

Visualize this. Am I having a conversation with John over Zoom? Am I having lunch with my friends? Am I walking up and down New York streets? Am I looking at art galleries? Who am I with? How am I ambulating? When I visualize this, I'm visualizing it out 30, 40 years. I want to live to 125. That's my number. I have to do preparatory work now to get there tomorrow.

You talked about healthy longevity, but I want to add one more piece, which is quality of life. The WHO (World Health Organization) published a statistic that most people live their last 16 years of life with two chronic diseases. I want to fly over that. I do not want to land in any of those camps, so I am doing everything I can that's available to me. I'm not in a laboratory or something like that. There are social media influencers out there that are truly human lab rats. They're experimenting with themselves as test subjects and pouring in millions of dollars annually to do so. They're experimenting for us. We are all learning.

I believe you need to think about how far out you want to be living. I think everybody would concur that quality of life matters because everyone at this age has experienced the opposite. That, to me, is a financial risk, just like you're talking about in terms of long-term care. These are all the hidden costs that nobody calculates. When I talk about my non-financial finance part of my program, that's a huge cost that people aren't even aware of.

John Creekmur: What is one piece of advice you'd give somebody who is heading to that retirement stage, and they're seeking to make the most out of that next chapter?

Nancy Schwartz: Reboot your energy levels!

NANCY SCHWARTZ

Nancy Schwartz is the Founder and Principal of Envision Healthy Retirement. With a background in corporate leadership, she founded the retained search company SearchExecution and served as a Client Partner at Korn Ferry, where she worked with industries ranging from global multinationals to early-stage private equity. Known for her innovative, solution-driven approach, Nancy has earned recognition for tackling complex challenges.

A classically trained ballerina, Nancy has performed with renowned ballet and modern dance companies. She has built several professional dance companies and a nonprofit dance studio, fostering creativity and inclusion in choreography. Passionate about personal growth, she is a certified Health and Lifestyle Consultant, with credentials from Tiny Habits®, Retirement Options, HeartMath, and the Health Coach Institute. A Skidmore College graduate, Nancy remains actively involved in mentorships focused on health and business.

web | www.EnvisionHealthyRetirement.com
email | Nancy.schwartz@envisionhealthyretirement.com
phone | (917) 733 - 9182

TERRY TUCKER

Embracing Everyday: A Story of Hope

YOUR BLUEPRINT FOR PURPOSE

YOU HAVE DONE IT ALL. You have performed at the top of your game. Achievement and impact are seen. Yet life happens. What do you do? We have all been there. We do not understand. Why did this happen? Doubts creep in, you may get discouraged and distracted.

Don't go it alone. Look to others that are experiencing their own journey.

Terry is one such person. High-achiever throughout his entire life, impact in numerous fields and in numerous ways- personally, professionally, familiarly, in his community. Yet the ability to achieve often times is not set in ability, it is founded in perspective.

As you have been building yoru own incredible life, take time to develop your perspective. Center your actions on a firm foundation. When the winds of life blow, it is the foundation that will keep your plans grounded, and moving to an incredible life.

🎙 SCAN ME TO LISTEN TO TERRY'S FULL INTERVIEW

John Creekmur: Terry, to start, can you give us a bit of your background?

Terry Tucker: I grew up on the South Side of Chicago. I'm the oldest of three boys. You can't tell from my voice, but I'm six foot, eight inches tall, and went to college at the Citadel in Charleston, South Carolina on an athletic scholarship to play basketball despite having three knee surgeries in high school. When I graduated from college, I moved home to find a job. I'm really going to date myself now, but this was long before the Internet was available to help people find employment. Fortunately, I found that first job in the corporate headquarters of Wendy's International, the hamburger chain, in their marketing department. That was the good news. The bad news was I lived with my parents for the next three and a half years as I helped my mother care for my father and my grandmother, who were both dying of different forms of cancer.

Eventually, I moved to hospital administration. I actually went to work for the hospital that cared for my father and my grandmother. Then, I made a major pivot in my life and became a police officer. One of the positions I held during my law enforcement career was a SWAT hostage negotiator. After that, I started a school security consulting business, and coached girls high school basketball when we lived in Texas. But for the last 12 years now, I have been battling a rare form of melanoma. My wife and I have been married for almost 31 years. We have one child, a daughter who is a graduate of the United States Air Force Academy and is an officer in the new branch of the military, The Space Force.

John Creekmur: It's amazing how far technology has come. You too have had a lot of transformations over the course of your career. You mentioned that you were a SWAT hostage negotiator. How did you transition into that role?

Terry Tucker: SWAT teams, regardless of the type of law enforcement agency, are usually the best officers with the best training and the best equipment. I've always wanted to be part of the best in my life, so when there was an opening for a person on the negotiating team, I put in for it. I had to do the physical fitness part of it, running a mile and doing pushups and sit-ups. I had to meet with the psychologist and take psychological exams. I met with the command staff and then met with the team.

When it came to the team, it was all-or-nothing. If everybody gave you a thumbs up, you got on the team. If one person said no, you didn't make it. I was fortunate enough to get a thumbs-up from everybody on the team. That started a four-and-a-half-year odyssey of being in some exciting situations, getting some excellent training, working with amazing people, and hopefully making a difference in people's lives.

John Creekmur: You went from that to coaching girls' high school basketball. That's another incredible change. I know you were also doing security consulting with schools at that time, so you were bringing that military background. But when you think about the different varied experiences you have had, how has that influenced your perspective?

Terry Tucker: I've been very fortunate. My parents taught my brothers and me the importance of family, of loving each other, caring for each other, and supporting each other. We were all athletes. My youngest brother was a pitcher for the University of Notre Dame. My middle brother was an NCAA Division II All-American and was drafted by the Cleveland Cavaliers of the National Basketball Association. We're all well over six feet tall, so we used to joke that if you sat behind our family in church, there wasn't a prayer's chance you were going to see anything in front of you. But our five-foot-eight-inch mother was the boss. It didn't matter how big, tall, or strong we were; whatever mom said, that was the way it went.

My parents taught us that everybody was important and everybody mattered. That was an incredibly important thing when I was a negotiator and a police officer. You may pull somebody over as a police officer, and you have to keep in mind that it may be the scariest thing that happens to them all year. For you, it's the third traffic stop of the night. You have to keep that in perspective.

It's the same thing with negotiating. One of the things that we used to do to try to change behavior is what we called tactical empathy. You can get rid of the word tactical and just use empathy. Empathy means, help me understand where you're coming from, even if I don't necessarily agree with it. If I'm negotiating with a homicide suspect, I'm not going to agree with the fact that murdering somebody was a good thing. But I want to understand where you're coming from because empathy builds trust, and trust gets to a point where you can change behavior. As negotiators, that's exactly what we were trying to do: change people's behavior because let's face it, if you're talking to me and your house is surrounded by the police, you're probably having the worst day of your life.

John Creekmur: For sure. I think empathy is such a big word, and it's such a big concept to live by. It's trying to understand the circumstances of life an individual is walking through. I've learned when I work with couples and their finances to really have empathy concerning their backgrounds and the things they've walked through.

Empathy is such a critical thing. I encourage you to do some additional reading on empathy because it is a life changer. It's not just for hostage negotiations; it's for everyday things of life.

I was thinking of another word: resilience. I know you've had a 12-year journey with cancer. That's a long journey, and you're such a positive individual. You're always smiling and laughing. Can you share how your battle with cancer has impacted your outlook on life moving forward?

Terry Tucker: Sure. I was diagnosed with a rare form of melanoma, and most people think of melanoma as too much exposure to the sun. My form has nothing to do with sun exposure. It's a rare type that appears on the bottom of the feet or the palms of the hands. Mine appeared on the bottom of my foot. This was back in 2012, and I was told when I was diagnosed that more than likely I would be dead in two years. They had nothing to offer me in terms of treatment other than surgery. If they could cut it out, they would. Otherwise, there was nothing they could do for me.

I thought, "Well, you've given me a death sentence. Maybe I can try to turn that death sentence into a life sentence." And that's what I've been trying to do for the last almost 12 years now.

I was on a medication for five years that gave me severe flu-like symptoms every week after I took the injection. I had the flu every week for five years. As my oncologist used to say, "That's not a cure. We're just trying to kick the can down the road for you." I had my foot amputated in 2018. I had my leg amputated in 2020, and I still have tumors in my lungs, which I'm being treated for. I get the question a lot, "You were a college athlete, you were in law enforcement, you did a lot of physical things in your life. How do you reconcile the fact that you're in a wheelchair, you don't have a leg and you still have tumors in your lungs?" My response to that is, "When you can't do what you were good at, you do what's important."

That's what I've been trying to do for 12 years. Certainly, since I've had my leg amputated, my life has significantly changed. You get to a point where you understand what's important in life. Was playing basketball important in the scheme of things? Not really. Being in law enforcement, I probably helped some people, but now my purpose is to put goodness, positivity, motivation, and love back into the world with whatever time I have left. That's being resilient. Being on the show with you and getting to talk to you, that energizes me, that gives me the drive to continue to move forward. I'm treated at the hospital every three weeks, for the entire week, for the tumors in my lungs. I get these two-week cycles off, and having conversations with you gives me a reason to keep going on.

John Creekmur: What a great message: that pursuit of excellence in every area of your life, regardless of the circumstances. That brings me to your book, *Sustainable Excellence*. What made you choose that title, and what are some of the core principles of the book?

Terry Tucker: I never set out to write a book. As a matter of fact, I really poo-pooed it. There's an old joke that says, "When we talk to God, it's called prayer. When God talks to us, it's called schizophrenia." God has never talked to me in any way, shape, or form about writing a book. But I believe God put enough people in my life who kept making the same suggestion: "Terry, you should write a book, Terry, you should write a book." I always say, "I wrote the book, but it was inspired by something bigger than me."

People always ask me, "Well, what is excellence?" My response is, "I don't know. Kind of like beauty, I think excellence is in the eye of the beholder."

You have to define for yourself what excellence looks like in your life, but then how do you sustain it? How do you get to a point where you continue to grow? I've seen people do this; they get to the top of the mountain, and then they sit back and put their feet up on the desk and say, "You know what? I've arrived. I've made it." A year later, somebody passes them up, and they say, "What happened?"

What happened was you didn't grow, you didn't innovate, you didn't find new ways to deliver your service. How do you continue to sustain, to grow, to get better? That's sustainable excellence in a nutshell. The principles were developed based on a young man who reached out to me on social media and said, "What do you think are the most important things I should learn not to just be successful in my job or business but to be successful in life?" I didn't want to give him the cliches that we all know. I wanted to see if I could go deeper, so I took some time and took some notes, and eventually developed these 10 principles.

I sent them to him, and then I stepped back and said, "I've got a life story that fits underneath that principle." During the months I was healing after I had my leg amputated, I sat down at the computer and I built stories. They're real stories about real people underneath each of the principles. That's how *Sustainable Excellence* came to be. I'll give you a couple of the principles. One of them is very important to me because I've done it in my life, and I'm not proud to say that I have done it.

Most people think with their fears and their insecurities instead of using their minds. I know I've done that in my life. I wanted to start something, but I thought, "Maybe I'm not smart enough, or maybe I don't have enough information. What will people say about me if I fail?" That's thinking with our fears and our insecurities, not our minds.

When I have an opportunity to talk to young people, I always tell them, "If there's something in your heart that you believe you're supposed to do, but it scares you, go ahead and do it, because, at the end of your life, the things you're going to regret are not going to be those things you did. They're going to be those things you didn't do. By then, it's too late."

John Creekmur: That is a key principle. I think everyone can relate to that. You have 10 principles in the book, correct?

Terry Tucker: Yes. A lot of them have to do with things I've learned over my life. There's one about being curious. We were always taught as negotiators to use a curious voice when we were talking with people and to slow down. It really is more about being a lifelong learner. I want to be one of those people who is always obtaining more knowledge. I want to die learning. I don't ever want to think, "Hey, I know it all. I've got it all figured out," because I'm in my 60s and I haven't figured it all out.

John Creekmur: I love the lifelong learner. It's a principle we taught to our own kids for so many years. I love that phrase, "Be curious." In your 60s, you've gone through a lot in life. Can you walk through how people can continue to find opportunities for personal growth when they go through retirement?

Terry Tucker: I think you need to start with the understanding that there's no such thing as a perfect job, a perfect person, or a perfect relationship. There's no such thing as perfect. If you're looking for something perfect, you're going to be sorely disappointed. We all have unique gifts and talents that were given to us by our Creator. Use those gifts and talents. Try new things. Jesse Itzler, who is the husband of Sarah Blakely, who started Spanx, which is a woman's undergarment company, said, "She started that company with one prototype and $5,000 and didn't know all kinds of things about starting a business." But the point of his story is that if she would've waited until everything lined up perfectly, somebody else would've figured that idea out and run with it.

You have to jump in with both feet, figure it out as you grow, make mistakes, and learn from those mistakes. I love the quote from Nelson Mandela, who said, "I never lose. I either learn or I win." Understand that the road to success is paved with failure. You're going to have to make mistakes, but mistakes are only bad if you don't learn from them. Learn the things you're supposed to learn by trying new things.

We get paralyzed. We don't know where to begin. Right where you are is a perfectly fine place to start. Just jump in and figure it out as you go.

Don't say, "I've got to wait until this happens." Start right now. Whatever will happen will happen. I always like the saying that goes, "Whatever happens to you has been waiting to happen to you since the beginning of time."

Understand that things are going to happen, good and bad. You've got to understand you have unique gifts and talents. Use those for the betterment of yourself and your community and see where your life goes. I'll end with this quick story. Most of us know Mr. Rogers, the host of the public television show, *Mr. Roger's Neighborhood*. He educated so many young people, including me. When Fred Rogers died in 2003, his family was going through his effects and they found his wallet. Inside his wallet was a scrap piece of paper on which Mr. Rogers had written four simple words, "Life is for service." Use your gifts in service of others.

John Creekmur: I had never heard that before. Life is for service. Can you, in closing, give us any key thoughts or principles you want to leave with people to help them make great decisions and live incredible lives?

Terry Tucker: Let me end with another story. I've always been a big fan of Westerns. When I was young, my mom and dad would let me stay up late and watch *Bonanza* and *Gun Smoke*. My favorite was *Wild Wild West*. In 1993, the movie *Tombstone* was released. It was a huge blockbuster. It starred Val Kilmer as a man by the name of John "Doc" Holliday and Kurt Russell as a man by the name of Wyatt

Earp. Now, Doc Holliday and Wyatt Earp were two living, breathing human beings who walked on the face of the earth. They're not made-up characters just for the movie. Doc was called Doc because he was a dentist by trade, but he was also a gunslinger and a card shark, and Wyatt Earp had been some form of a lawman almost his entire life.

Somehow, these two men from entirely opposite backgrounds formed this incredibly close friendship. At the end of the movie, Doc Holliday is dying at a sanitarium in Glenwood Springs, Colorado, which is about three hours from where I live. The real Doc Holliday died at that sanitarium. He's buried in the Glenwood Springs Cemetery. Wyatt, at this point in his life, is destitute. He has no money, no job, and no prospects for a job, so every day he comes to play cards with Doc, and the two men pass the time that way. In almost the last scene of the movie, they're talking about what they want out of life. Doc says, "I was in love with my cousin when I was young, but she joined a convent over the affair. She's all that I ever wanted." Then, he looks at Wyatt and says, "What about you, Wyatt? What do you want?"

Wyatt nonchalantly says, "I just want to lead a normal life." And Doc looks at him and says, "There's no normal; there's just life. Get on with living yours."

There are probably people reading this who are sitting back and saying, "When this happens, I'll have a normal life. When that occurs, I'll have a successful life." I'd like to tell those people this: Don't wait for life to come to you. Get out there and find the reason you were put on the face of this earth. Use your unique gifts and talents and live that reason, because if you do, at the end of your life, you're going to be a whole lot happier, and you're going to have a whole lot more peace in your heart.

Terry Tucker is a motivational speaker, author and international podcast guest on the topics of motivation, mindset and self-development.

He holds a business degree from The Citadel (where he played NCAA Division I college basketball) and a master's degree from Boston University. In his professional career, Terry has been a marketing executive, a hospital administrator, a SWAT Team Hostage Negotiator, a high-school basketball coach, a business owner, a motivational speaker and for the past twelve years, a cancer warrior (which has resulted in the amputation of his foot in 2018 and his leg in 2020).

He is the author of the book, *Sustainable Excellence: Ten Principles to Leading Your Uncommon and Extraordinary Life*. Terry has also been featured in *Authority*, *Thrive Global* and *Human Capital Leadership* magazines, along with being quoted and featured in the new book, *Audaciousness: Your Journey to Living a Bold and Authentic Life* by Maribel Ortega and Helen Strong.

web | www.motivationalcheck.com
email | motivationalcheck@aol.com

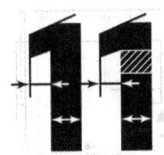

SCOTT WITZIG

Gathering, Growing, & Granting for Community Impact

YOUR BLUEPRINT FOR PURPOSE

ALL THAT WE SEE AND DO IN LIFE, is built upon those that have gone before. A classic principle that others living an incredible life have contributed to the life that you lead. What do we learn from them? How have they impacted us, our communities, our families, the things that we hold dear?

At times we get to a point when we have a strong desire to impact others, yet we are not certain of the next steps. Steps may seem overwhelming, and daunting, yet do not have to be. All it takes is to have a guide. Someone whose life has been driven by a desire to shepherd others in the journey of impact.

Scott brings so much to helping people in living out and executing their true impact goals. Driving change, changing lives, and living an incredible life.

🎙 SCAN ME TO LISTEN TO SCOTT'S FULL INTERVIEW

SCOTT WITZIG

John Creekmur: Scott Witzig is the executive director of the Morton Community Foundation in Morton, Illinois. Scott, can you tell us about your background?

Scott Witzig: I have a very circuitous career path. My family owned a clothing business here in Morton for 84 years. My great-great-grandfather was a tailor, and he started a little tailoring shop here in town which my dad and his brother continued and grew until my cousin, my brother and I came into the business.

I spent the first 17 years of my work life in the family business, and I loved that work. But, as family clothing stores kind of went down the path of extinction, I ended up taking a job as Executive Director of the Morton Chamber of Commerce back in about 1992. I spent four and a half years there until a friend of mine who ran a meat processing company here in Morton asked me to come work for him as marketing director. He was developing a new, fully cooked meat entree product, and he needed somebody to help him market it, which was a weird twist for me, going from the clothing business to the meat industry.

But we had a lot of success, and we grew the company to the point where the company was bought out by Smithfield Foods out in Smithfield, Virginia. I told John, "Before somebody at headquarters out there tells me to leave, I'd better start looking for a job. They don't really need marketing directors when they have an $11 billion company."

I started to put feelers out in the community. The Morton Community Foundation was in its infancy. It had started in 2000, and they started to try to really make this thing grow because volunteers were unable to invest the time it takes to build the endowments.

The Board wanted somebody to come in, be the first staff person and wake up every morning with the idea of, how can I grow this organization? I applied for that job and was hired as executive director in the year of 2007. That's how I got here. I'm married; I have four children and five grandchildren. I've lived in Morton my whole life, and I love this community and working with people who have a passion for charitable causes in our community.

John Creekmur: It's interesting. Back when I was a sophomore in college, I was sitting in the Morton Federal Savings and Loan Bank in downtown Morton, Illinois. It's a town of about 20,000 people right now, and community is such a huge part of the incredible fabric of this community. I was sitting there talking to a dear friend of our family, Ed Hauter, and I believe you have a little connection with Ed. He said, "John, you need to head over to Witzig's and get you a nice-looking suit for whenever you go to meet with business people." I got my first business suit from your family store.

Scott Witzig: Ed Hauter—Uncle Ed—is married to Shirley (Witzig) Hauter, who was my dad's sister. That's the connection there.

John Creekmur: Morton, Illinois is right at the center of the state, so if you ever get a chance during the month of September, you should make your way out to the Morton Pumpkin Festival, which is a phenomenal community event.

SCOTT WITZIG

Scott Witzig: When I was Director of the Chamber of Commerce, one of my responsibilities was planning and presenting the Morton Pumpkin Festival. For four and a half years, I was in charge of that. Even today, so many people see me at the pumpkin festival and ask me, "How's it going? Is it a busy one? Are we doing well?" I tell them, "I don't really know because I'm not that involved in it." Of course, they think I'm still in charge, so they kind of chuckle and say, "Yeah, right. I'm sure." I try not to get into too much detail, because I'd be answering questions with lots of people. But it was an interesting thing to be in charge of.

John Creekmur: I'm always surprised at the number of volunteers there are. It's a very big festival, with many people coming through.

Scott Witzig: I think they say 100,000 people. There's really no way to count. Our office is essentially right in the middle of the Midway, so we're surrounded with equipment and generators and Midway games, it's exciting.

John Creekmur: It speaks to how the community gives back in so many different ways. One of the ways I've seen over the years is the number of people who have served on the board of the Morton Community Foundation and who also have set up grants through the Morton Community Foundation. Can you walk our readers through what a community foundation does?

Scott Witzig: We like to use three words: gather, grow and grant. It's the easiest way to capsulize what we do. We *gather* tax deductible donations because we're a 501(c)(3) organization. We can accept donor gifts that are deductible. We take those donations, and we invest, or *grow*, them in the market. From the proceeds of those investments, we give *grants*, and those grants are distributed according to the various funds we have. There are over 100 different endowment funds we hold here, and each of those endowments are specifically designated by donors as to how they would like the grants to be distributed.

John Creekmur: Let's unpack all three of those words, starting with "gather." If somebody comes to you, and they'd like to in some way participate in the foundation, is that something where they would simply bring in their loose change around the house? Is that a check? Is that appreciated stock? Is that land? What can they give as a donation to the 501(c)(3)?

Scott Witzig: Because we have over 100 individual endowed funds already in existence, a person could literally just walk in with $5 and say, "I would like to put this $5 in the Morton Fine Arts Endowment." Every fund becomes a public charitable fund available for any donor to give to, and all those funds sit under the 501(c)(3) charitable umbrella of the Morton Community Foundation. A person can donate to any of those 100 funds. They could also donate to the Morton Community Foundation itself to support the operations of the MCF. You can walk in with cash or a check. You can donate using a credit card; you can donate online. You can choose a fund from our website and can donate $10, $25, $100—whatever you want.

But if you wanted to establish your own endowment fund to benefit your favorite causes or charities, you would make a commitment of a minimum of $10,000. That $10,000 doesn't have to be donated all at once. You could start with as little as $1,000 with a commitment of donating an additional $1,000 each year until you've reached your $10,000. At the point that the fund hits $10,000 by the end of a given fiscal year, then the following spring, it would generate its first grant to the cause for which the fund was established. We call it an acorn fund, because you're planting the seeds along the way until you get to the $10,000.

There are so many ways to give, of course cash, credit card, or check. But we are also able to accept more complex gifts, like gifts of highly appreciated stock, where the donor transfers shares of highly appreciated stock. Donors may transfer that stock directly to our account, we can liquidate it at no cost to us, and the donor doesn't pay capital gains tax on the appreciation of the stock value.

At age 70 1/2, a qualified charitable distribution from their IRA can be directly transferred into any of the endowed funds held at the Morton Community Foundation and the donor would pay no income tax on those funds. At age 73, donors have a required minimum distribution (RMD) obligation every year. They would normally pay income tax on any distribution received personally, but if the donor transfers some or all of their RMD directly to the community foundation (or any other 501(c)(3) or charitable equivalent), they don't have to pay that income tax on the portion transferred to the charity.

Farmers should check with their tax accountant as there are significant tax benefits for them to donate bushels of grain directly to a charity. And, we can also accommodate donations of farmland directed to the Morton Community Foundation.

John Creekmur: Pretty much wherever a person is sitting at financially, they have a way to participate with a community foundation in some way, whether it be by establishing their own program or their own account or partnering with somebody who has already been established in some way. They can donate stock as appreciated. They can donate other appreciated assets. They can probably change the beneficiary on a life insurance policy to the foundation. It sounds like that's an easy way for folks to really make an impact in their local communities.

Scott Witzig: Yes, and the final example would be setting us up as a beneficiary of a portion of their estate through a will. Some donors have set up their will so that upon their passing, a fund is established at the community foundation. It could be really beneficial to the family of the estate to distribute their IRA to the community foundation because then the family doesn't have to pay the income tax on that IRA. In other words, if there were options, they would rather donate their IRA than give, say, their house as an asset.

John Creekmur: You mentioned the second phase is to grow the account. Once the dollars are received into the foundation, then you guys have to go and invest those dollars in a prudent way. Is there a lot of risk that dollars won't be paid out to people? Walk through the way you make sure their dollars actually grow over time.

Scott Witzig: Since the foundation started, we've been partnered with the Community Foundation of Central Illinois in Peoria. It used to be called the Peoria Area Community Foundation. I believe they currently have about $75 million invested. We're about $13.1 million of that. They take care of the investments. We pay them .5%

annually to do that work for us. That leaves me to be the spokesman for explaining the power of endowment, the difference between giving a direct gift to a nonprofit versus endowing a gift, which will then last forever. Of that investing, the Community Foundation of Central Illinois has an Investment Policy, which the MCF has adopted as well. That investment policy is set up to have 60% of the investments in the market, so to speak, and then 40% in fixed-income-type investments. That protects us from the huge market slings.

The other thing we do to help protect the principal, because our goal is giving grants to the charities the donor has chosen, is we have a Spending Policy that dictates that we'll calculate 5% of the four-year rolling average balance in that fund. That allows the fund to have years where the investment returns aren't quite as strong to cover that 5% plus our management fee, which is 1.5%. We need about a 6.5% long-term investment result in order to cover that. In some years, you're not going to hit that; other years, you're going to be way beyond that. Rather than spend the actual available funds, we average four years.

John Creekmur: A lot of it is making sure the money is there to fulfill the wishes of those that are making the donations, have been paid out to those that have benefited in the community. Speaking of which, I know you have over 100 different endowments. The husband of long-time employee at Creekmur Wealth Advisors, Brenda Geiger, passed away a couple of years ago, and I know that their family partnered with you on setting up a grant. I know a lot of people partner with you to make an impact in the community. Are there a couple of different endowments you would want to highlight to help people understand the practical ways they can make an impact on things that are important to them?

Scott Witzig: Sure. You mentioned Brenda Geiger. As you can imagine, often, my connection to a donor starts around the time they've had some sort of loss in the family. It's such an honor to be able to work with someone at a time when they're really hurting and they want to do something that leaves a legacy for their loved one.

With Brenda's husband passing, we set up a scholarship fund. Every year, on the first Monday in May, I go to the high school awards night, and we read the stories of the individuals who have scholarship funds set up in their memory. Not all scholarship fund holders feel comfortable in front of an auditorium, but Brenda comes up and reads the story about her husband, what he was like, what he loved to do, and why she established the scholarship in his name. It's a beautiful time to work with folks and hopefully help them to do something they really want to do.

I'll give you a couple other examples. We had a board member whose mother passed away many years ago, and she loved animals, so he set up, upon her passing, two endowments. One is for TAPS, the Tazewell Animal Protection Society, to support the work they do because that's what his mom would've loved. The other is called the Critter Meals on Wheels Endowment Fund. In Peoria, there's a nonprofit organization called Neighborhood House, and they do a Meals on Wheels program for senior citizens.

Every weekday, they're taking meals to these seniors. Some of the delivery people had been noticing that on occasion, they'd noticed that the Senior's pets were staying nice and plump and healthy while the individual senior citizen kept getting thinner and thinner. So, they started to ask questions: Are you eating your meals? And the senior would say, "I do eat my meals, but on Fridays, I know I'm not going to get another meal until Monday, so I set aside a portion of my meal for my pets to eat over the weekend to make sure they stay well-fed." That told them they needed to solve the problem of people going hungry because they're feeding their people food to the animals.

They started this Critter Meals on Wheels program where, in addition to the senior citizens receiving meals for themselves, they would receive a package of pet food for the dog, the cat or the birds. This endowment fund sends an annual grant to Neighborhood House to help purchase the pet food they use in their Critter Meals on Wheels program. It's touching to think how there are so many ways we can help others, and sometimes it's in a unique way you just wouldn't have thought was out there.

John Creekmur: It's a tangible thing that's having a huge impact in society. We know quality food is such a huge need for so many of our seniors. To think that a lot of them are sacrificing their own nutrition to take care of their animals is heartbreaking.

Scott Witzig: Yes, it is. I mentioned that this donor set up a TAPS Fund and Critter Meals on Wheels in memory of his mother. That TAPS Fund recently received a $75,000 estate gift from an individual who passed away, and they knew that there was a TAPS Fund endowment, so they gave a portion of their estate to that TAPS endowment. That fund instantly grew by a significant amount of money, so it'll be able to do even more for TAPS. Once we set up a fund, the next person doesn't have to create their own thing; they can give to one that exists currently.

Here's another cool example. There was a lady who lived in Morton, but when she got her education, she became a teacher and moved away, and her entire career was spent somewhere in Northern Illinois. But then, after she retired, she moved back to Morton. Anyway, in her estate plan, she wanted to support eight of her favorite charities that she had been supporting during her lifetime. She wanted to give a little bit more to some of them than to others. Her attorney had been on our board for a number of years, so he understood how everything worked. He helped his client include language in her will that established an endowment upon her passing that generates annual grants that are divided into 11 equal shares. These eight separate charities receive either two shares or one share every year forever, and these charities happen to be all located outside of Morton.

If you work with the Morton Community Foundation, you don't just have to give to Morton based charities. You can support your favorite causes wherever they might be located. We would love for some of them to be local, but even if they're not, we love to work with those donors anyway, because holding their endowment does help our operations through the management fee we earn on those investments. This particular fund gives annual grants to two different public broadcasting radio stations, one in Bloomington, one in Champaign. It gives to the Peoria Riverfront Museum and the Peoria Symphony Orchestra, Unity Point Health Hospice, Peoria, the Alzheimer's Association (Peoria Chapter), the Dickson Mounds Museum and the Crazy Horse Memorial Foundation in South Dakota.

That fund is so interesting because we're sending these eight checks all around us and then all the way out to South Dakota. Dickson Mounds and Crazy Horse are two charities involved in Native American history. I thought, "I wonder why she chose those two." It turns out she grew up here in town, and her grandpa was a farmer, and they would take walks in a field to pick up rocks, and oftentimes they would find arrowheads from Native Americans, so she started having this passion for saving beads and arrowheads and different artifacts like that. She always loved Native American things, so in her endowment fund, she still supports them.

John Creekmur: That's amazing. Scott, is there anything we have not covered that you think would be pertinent for our readers?

Scott Witzig: We didn't talk much about that last word, "grants," but in general, we did talk about grants when we talked about the funds. Our Annual Community Grants are the part of our grant-making that most people are aware of. They occur every Spring. Those grants are generated from our Morton Impact Fund, which is an unrestricted endowment that allows us to request from all of our schools, the parks, the library and all the non-profits to submit applications for grant funding from this particular set of funds. That's the most visible. Last year, we distributed about $75,000 in community grants through this process. In the Spring of 2024, our fund has grown enough that we're going to be distributing about $91,000, and the next year it'll be over $100,000.

Our Community Grants continue to grow. But as I said, we have about $13.1 million invested, and we're spending 5% of the 4-year average balance of all of our endowment funds. As you can imagine, our distributions are much higher than the $75,000 most people hear about. That's because we have these 100 funds that have been predefined by their donors. By far, the biggest portion of our grantmaking is done automatically, where we send a check for this fund and we send eight checks for that fund. Last year, we distributed over $450,000 through those types of funds, so the MCF is an organization that is really starting to hit its stride, and it's kind of like a big snowball rolling, and it is just a beautiful thing to watch.

SCOTT WITZIG

Scott Witzig became the first paid Executive Director of the Morton Community Foundation in 2007, since it was founded in 2000 – guiding it into the future using his extensive community leadership in both the nonprofit and private sectors.

He received a bachelor's degree in Business Administration from Illinois State University in 1982. While at the Morton Chamber of Commerce, he attended annual training courses at the Leadership Institute at the University of Colorado, Boulder. His previous career experience includes 17 years with his family's clothing business, four and a half years as Executive Director of the Morton Chamber of Commerce and 10 years as Marketing Director for RMH Foods.

Scott's volunteer work has included leadership and involvement with many local organizations, and he was the recipient of the 2013 Morton Chamber of Commerce Distinguished Service Award.

web | www.mortoncommunityfoundation.org
email | switzig@mortoncommunityfoundation.org
phone | (309) 291 - 0434, (309) 696 - 1919

STEPHANIE ZEPEDA, Ph.D, LMFT-S

Building Trust & Financial Transparency

YOUR BLUEPRINT FOR PURPOSE

WHAT DO YOU DO WHEN no matter the discussions, planning, alignment of goals and actions steps, just get derailed. When no matter where you turn, no matter how intentional you are, there always seems to be an impediment. Maybe misalignment of core values in your marriage relationships. Maybe behaviors that are damaging to trust injuring the incredible life journey.

We all have been there form time to time. Stage of life bumps. Difficulty talking through important core items. Challenges that we continue to fail in. The focus on the hurts and the failures takes away from the hope and joy.

Stephanie shares in great detail the top ways that our actions and thoughts can derail our goals. What steps we need to take to get back on track. How to go from hurt to hope.

Often times, it seems scary to have deep talks, but by doing so, the journey becomes clearer.

SCAN ME TO LISTEN TO STEPHANIE'S FULL INTERVIEW

STEPHANIE ZEPEDA, Ph.D, LMFT-S

John Creekmur: Stephanie Zepeda is a marriage and family therapist specializing in financial therapy. Stephanie, can you explain what financial therapy is and how it's different from traditional financial planning or wealth management?

Stephanie Zepeda: This is one of the number one questions I get from people, because it's a relatively new field. The Financial Therapy Association started in 2010. It's combining those aspects of financial planning with the aspects of psychotherapy. The problem with the field of financial therapy is that sometimes you don't know what focus your financial therapist has. Sometimes, it's folks from the financial world who wanted to understand the therapeutic stuff a bit more, so they went and got a little bit of training in therapy. Sometimes, it's people from the therapy world who wanted to understand the financial stuff better so they went and got more training in the financial side. When you are looking for a financial therapist, do a little research. The Financial Therapy Association is a great place to start.

If you're wanting more financial planning and you want someone who understands the psychology of it, go with a financial planning person who has financial therapy training. If you're needing more communication help or relationship help, look for a financial therapist who has more of the psychological training. If you're looking in particular for help with your marriage, help with your relationship with your children, you want to look for a licensed marriage and family therapist who has training in financial therapy, because it's the only field in the United States that has requirements in the training to have relational hours. All the other licenses are beautiful and wonderful, but they just have a slightly different focus.

Licensed marriage and family therapists are looking at the system. Often, clients say, "We have a financial planner who told us what to do. We can't do it. Why can't we do it? What's stopping us from doing this?" Often, it's that they haven't had those conversations they need to have, and that's what I help them do. Time and time again, they say, "Oh my God, I wish we had done this 10 years ago. I've been wanting to say this thing, and I didn't know how to say it in a way that wasn't horribly offensive or really going to hurt the other person." We can have those conversations, and it's beautiful to see the cascading effects that it has on the rest of the relationship.

John Creekmur: Is there a difference in how you walk through a conversation like that with people based upon those generations? Or do you see a lot of the similar principles that can be applied universally?

Stephanie Zepeda: People have similar money hangups across the generations. But millennials, Gen Zers and Gen Xers have a little bit more hopefulness of how to get out of the mess. I'm talking folks who maybe have built up quite a bit of credit card debt. I've had some folks come to me with six figures of credit card debt, and the younger you are, the more hopeful you are about getting out of that.

Folks who come to me at retirement age tend to have to do some work to get out of that hopelessness. They think there's no time to change. You can change two things: You can change the situation financially or you can change your mindset. With my younger-generation folks, we're working on both. With my folks who are already at retirement age, we're working more on mindset: What are the facts we've got here, and how can we shift you but still align with your values and virtues?

STEPHANIE ZEPEDA, Ph.D, LMFT-S

Maybe you're not going to hit these financial hopes and dreams you had. How can we mourn that and look at what we still have? What did you accomplish? What can you still accomplish? Life is not just about living well; it's about dying well. Your last thoughts as you leave this plane of existence hopefully aren't, "Man, I really regret that." Hopefully, they're, "Yeah, that was fun." We get very philosophical very quickly about how to live the rest of your life aligned with the values you hold most dear.

John Creekmur: That's interesting. Is the hopefulness the younger people have sometimes unrealistic? Is there a pragmatic way to walk through that?

Stephanie Zepeda: Generally, folks tend to be in one of two camps: Money is safety, and we need to guard it, or YOLO— money is to be spent because you don't know about tomorrow. They always marry each other. I think there's something really wise in that, because they need to marry each other. You need this person who's clinging too much to money to marry the person who can't hold onto it, because they help each other. But the YOLO mentality sometimes leads to over-hopefulness. They'll say, "We'll be fine. We'll always make more money. We're okay." Some of the pragmatic stuff is looking at the data together, and that's something I love about financial therapy.

We compared financial therapy to financial counseling before, but it's also different from traditional marriage therapy. In traditional marriage therapy, we're looking at the relationship, we're looking at the communication, we're looking at all these pieces and we're maybe not doing the pragmatic steps. Now, I don't do any investment advising. I refer to friends like you for that piece because I'm not a CPA. I'm not a

CFA. I leave that to others. But I do talk about where people have the most control in their budgets: discretionary spending, that fun money. My folks who are overly hopeful need a fun money budget. The person who is a little financially anxious and is clinging to money also needs fun money, because they never spend a dime because they think it's not safe.

I always ask, "Do you have fun money each month that you each get to spend?" The answer thus far has 100% of the time been, "No, we don't." The person who is terrified to spend money feels safe doing so because it's accounted for, and the person who is a little too hopeful also can spend safely because they say, "Okay, I know my limit." It's this beautiful boundary. They have boundaries in spending, but not where they're asphyxiated. It should feel limiting but not suffocating.

John Creekmur: Does some of the psychology change with that? Do some of their thoughts about money change? Is it different generationally?

Stephanie Zepeda: Every generation has fears. They might be for different reasons. One of the things we discuss on our intakes is family of origin. What were your money lessons you got from childhood, not just from your family but from your friends, from your culture, TV that you watched? It all informed our ideas of what we think we're supposed to do with our money, who we think is supposed to manage the money in a relationship, gender roles, all that stuff. The information feeding those money ideas changes from generation to generation, because the TV that a baby boomer watched is different than the TV that a Gen Zer watched, or a millennial.

I don't get too many people in their 20s. Sometimes, they're informed by TikTok or other social media. But I would say it really does categorize into, does money scare you, or do you kind of not think about it? That scarcity mindset versus abundance mindset. I actually don't like either of those mindsets. I like an ambivalence mindset that is both of those, because both of those mindsets have some very good parts to them. I think abundance mindset can be dangerous, and I think scarcity mindset is also dangerous, and we need to combine the two.

John Creekmur: A dear friend recently asked me something regarding financial values. He said, "We have different people from different backgrounds, and then we have in-laws that are coming into the mix with our kids getting married, and they have different backgrounds. How does one design this exact relationship with money that they desire? Is there a process to actually design it?" Is that something you've encountered? I often advise clients in similar situations to this, and I tell them to have weekly summits with their children to discuss things.

Stephanie Zepeda: Absolutely. I've got quite a few clients who have relationships in which one partner comes from generational wealth and the other partner does not. There are a lot of power dynamics that come into play. There can be suspicion of motive of the partner who's coming into the relationship who doesn't have as much money. In terms of creating a process, it has to come first and foremost from an investigation of the rules you've received about money from childhood and in your adult life.

I'm a millennial. Tons of financial trauma has happened to millennials generationally. How do we take all those money lessons and then have your partner list them, have your children list them? It must be so beautiful. I have a two-year-old and an eight-year-old. The eight-year-old already is getting money lessons from me, I can tell. It's so cool to see my eight-year-old and her development of her money ideas. I can imagine that seeing your adult children talk about what their money lessons were might be very challenging.

But might be really beautiful. We get them to where they can talk about which lessons they want to keep and which ones need to go in the garbage. Which ones were healthy and which ones were just weird and don't fit any more? Maybe they did fit once, but they don't fit any more. Then, what are the money values you would like to have that you don't quite have yet? What are some things you would like to change about your relationship with money?

One of the answers I hear the most is, "I want to understand it more. It freaks me out. I don't know how to do it. I want to understand." Conversely, others say, "I don't want to understand it at all. I just want to be told a number and that's it." Know your values and have a plan to maintain the ones you like and get rid of the ones you don't, and then to reach the ones you aspire towards.

John Creekmur: This is so interesting. Back in 1987, I was in the freshman year of my undergraduate program. I was taking a class called Worldviews whose professor was from Germany. He would sit there, and all of a sudden, he yelled out the word, "Weltanschauung." And I thought, "What are you talking about?" He said, "It's your world and life view." At the end of the day, what is it that is driving you down deep inside? What is your world-life view?

He said, "Let's take it away from that deep, stake-in-the-ground position. Let's examine those things that are core to you: your values, your character traits, your heritage, your legacy, those things that are really a sum of who you are. But now let's apply it to things like your view on money, your view on finances. Let's take it now and apply it to your view of how you live life, and how does that translate to how do you view people?"

I'm thinking now about clients specifically in that pre-retirement phase. I was talking recently with a couple who had some financial infidelity on one side of their relationship. They're heading to a change-of-life stage. With that change of life comes a lot more uncertainty. They used to work and now they don't. They're now going to seeing each other all the time. There's a lot of uncertainty, and then we have past financial differences and financial infidelity. When it comes to their world-life views about money, what steps would you give them as they walk through this conversation to identify what's important about money to them? How do they walk through that healing process?

Stephanie Zepeda: I love this topic of financial fidelity. Just like physical infidelity, people don't talk about what it means often. It's really common. There are multiple ways that you can have financial infidelity in your relationship. It can be hiding spending. It can be hiding income, where I have income, but I'm scared to tell my spouse about it because I'm afraid they're going to start dreaming, so to protect the family, I'm going to hide this. The intention behind financial infidelity can sometimes be good, but a lot of times I am seeing this come out with credit cards being opened that they didn't tell the other person about, loans being taken out, investments being made.

How do you rebuild trust after that is through transparency and setting up a loving accountability. You want a system where the person who committed the infidelity is held to account, but you don't want to crucify them, because that's just going to hurt the relationship even more. I've worked with folks who have had financial infidelity that's so crushing, especially around gambling addictions. Gambling is not legal in Texas, but sports betting is legal everywhere now because it's online. Then there are casinos and scratch-off tickets.

There's also day trading. The day-trading apps are little casinos in your pocket. It's gambling. It is gambling. You see this gambling behavior pop up. Sometimes, we have to get pretty structured with how we reestablish the trust and have transparency. It has to be done with consent. You would never do this behind your partner's back. In fact, you can't. You have to do it with their consent to get the passwords. But, for folks who admit they have problems, we do a detox.

Just like a detox from alcohol addiction, we do a detox from spending and they're put on an allowance with a debit card. For all the other accounts, the passwords are changed. The partner who does not have the spending or gambling problem changes the passwords. They freeze their credit so they can't take out credit. Both partners feel such safety in it. The partner who has the spending addiction or the gambling addiction feels safe that they're not going to fall again, and the partner who was left in the dark feels safe that their partner is not going to hurt the family finances. Now, if it's not a gambling issue, you might not need that extreme of a reaction.

But you do want to establish those roads of transparency and communication. How are we talking about our spending? I go back to that discretionary fund money I was talking about earlier. I wonder if this person who had the financial infidelity knew an amount they were supposed to be spending or not. I wonder about having standards and expectations for the family, especially when you're helping people transition from living on income to living on interest. It is scary, and I think having that clear plan and communication helps a lot. But again, I understand communication can be very frightening for people sometimes.

John Creekmur: It seems like once you get the plan in place, communication is key. If they don't have the communication, they're never going to walk through the challenge together.

Stephanie Zepeda: Exactly. It's not just about doing the detox and setting up the allowance. It's about working through, "Why did my brain go to that for stress relief? What am I replacing it with actively?" You can use that itch as an opportunity to connect. But if you don't feel safe going to your partner, it's a missed opportunity for connection. It's the retirement dream and hope. So many people situate it financially, and that's a big mistake.

You've got to situate it relationally. You have to be thinking about who you're marrying, who you're dating. I'm not saying don't have fun, but if you're wanting to settle down and plan your life with someone, make sure it's someone who you know will want to walk through the hard stuff of life with you. There's a reason we take marriage vows; because it's hard. If it were easy, we wouldn't have to take marriage vows. We wouldn't have to promise anything. It's really hard to walk through life with somebody. Neglecting your connection to the other person is just as bad as neglecting your stock portfolio. Taking that time has huge benefits, because not only does it help you build wealth better, but it also means that when you retire, you actually want to spend time with this person you've been planning for retirement with.

John Creekmur: Without that relationship, what does it matter how much money you have? Steph, do you have any parting thoughts you want to encourage folks with before we sign off today?

Stephanie Zepeda: I want to say that although we've talked about a lot of complicated stuff, and it might seem overwhelming, it's very hopeful. I have seen folks come back from such pain. It's never too late to change. Even if you're thinking, "This relationship is over. There's no good left in it," if you have a shred of hope, it can be enough to fill the entire relationship, so please hold onto that hope and be sure to reach out for help.

STEPHANIE ZEPEDA, Ph.D, LMFT-S

Stephanie Zepeda, Ph.D, LMFT-S, is a Marriage and Family Therapist specializing in Financial Therapy, particularly in helping couples navigate financial challenges during retirement planning.

With a PhD in Marriage & Family Therapy and Texas state licensure, she combines expertise and compassion to transform couples' lives.

Stephanie also serves as an associate professor at Our Lady of the Lake University, contributing to education and research in her field. Her mission is to foster financial harmony and emotional well-being in couples, making her a prominent figure in the realm of Financial Therapy.

web | www.FinancialTherapyTexas.com
email | DrZepeda@FinancialTherapyTexas.com

Next Steps

THANK YOU FOR READING THIS BOOK. I trust you found the interviews to be as informative, and thought-provoking as I did.

I hope this book showed you the importance of creating a blueprint for living your life and achieving your financial goals. My goal was to show you that it is possible to plan the future you want.

My intent was to empower you to create your blueprint and help you make smart financial decisions in your life.

If you have any follow up questions for any interview, feel free to reach out to each of the people in the book. Their contact information is at the end of their chapter.

Because your purchased this book, you can reach out to me for a complimentary consultation on how to start your blueprint and build the life you've always dreamed about. I will be happy to answer any questions you might have. If you decide to take advantage of this offer, my contact information is on the next page.

Let us help you start...

866-358-4441

www.CreekmurWealth.com

www.ingramcontent.com/pod-product-compliance
Lightning Source LLC
Chambersburg PA
CBHW052153220526
45471CB00004B/1663